THE LITTLE BOOK OF Cognac

Christian Pessey

Flammarion

C O N T

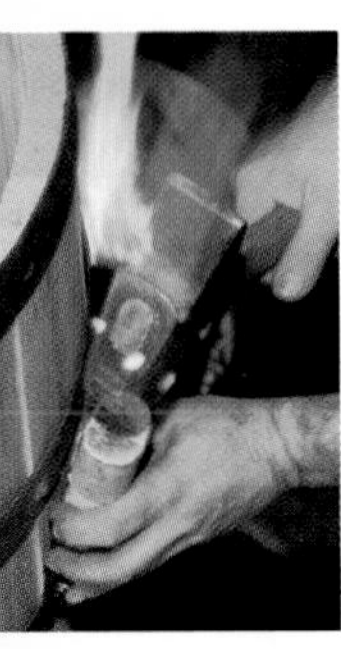

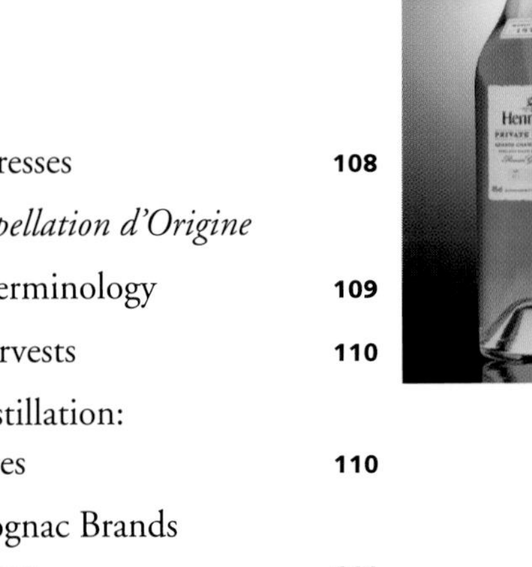

Alphabetical Guide

The alphabetical entries have been classified according to the following categories. The categories are indicated with a small colored rectangle.

The Land and The Vine

The People and Their Work

The Products

The information given in each entry, together with cross-references indicated by asterisks, enable the reader to explore the world of cognac.

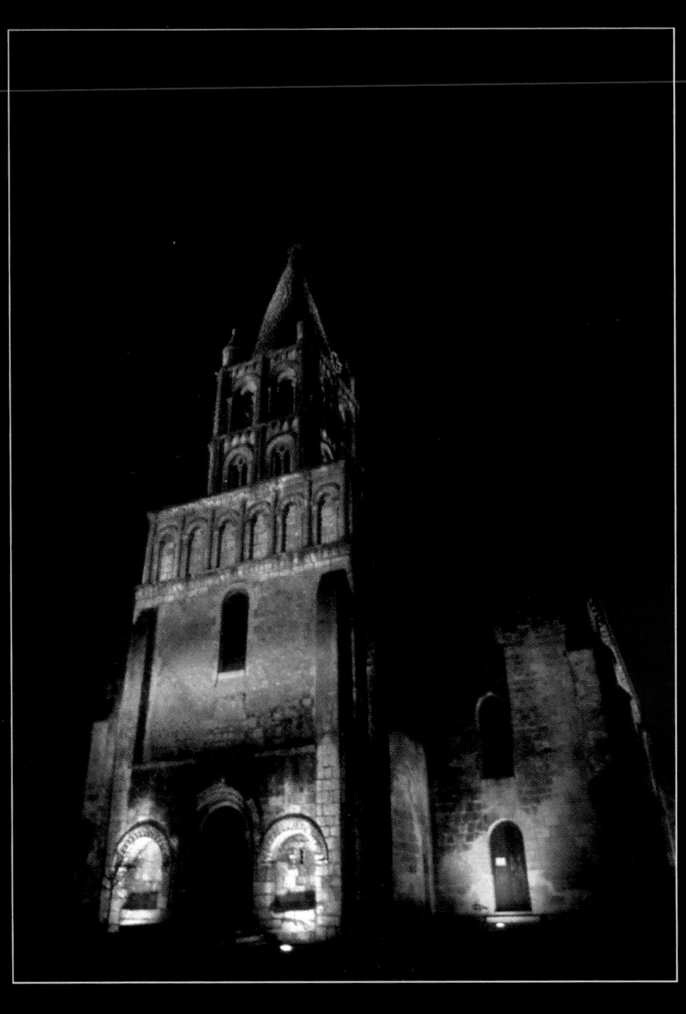

The church in Segonzac, the third most important cognac town.

THE STORY OF COGNAC

Celts, Gauls, and Francs

It was in the third century A.D. that the Celtic Santones planted vines in the fertile soil of the lands they occupied and to which they would lend their name, the Saintonge.

Under the emperor Augustus, the Romans colonized the region and established a capital at Saintes (whose founding is even attributed to the famous general, Agrippa). The region produced wine as early as the third century, when Emperor Probus granted all of Gaul the right to plant grapevines and produce wine. A good communications network—including the Roman Saintes–Lyon road or, more precisely, Mediolanum Santonum-Lugdunum, to use the inscription found on the milestones at the time—linked the region to the rest of Gaul, resulting in economic and cultural growth within the province. The area increased its contacts with the rest of Gaul and with Rome, to which the road from Saintes eventually led. The large road ran along the Charente* River, passed through Angoulême (known as Icalisma to the Santones, becoming Engolisma under the Romans), crossed the Massif Central mountain range, and dipped toward the Gallic capital. Soon, however, peaceful merchants and legionnaires, subdued by the pleasant climate*, were not the only ones to frequent the roads. Invasion followed invasion, and Saintonge found itself on the barbarians' route, as did the neighboring Angoumois and Aunis regions. Two events would stand out in the history of this region—in 507 the Frankish ruler Clovis pushed the Visigoths back to Vouillé, and in 732 Charles Martel stopped the Arabs at Poitiers.

Dolmen, Saint-Brice.

The well-situated region benefited from a very gentle climate and easy access to the sea by way of the, then navigable, Charente River. Charlemagne encouraged the growing of crops and grapevines in the region. The coastal salt marshes produced the region's "white gold," and were the point of departure for salt routes leading to numerous destinations. Northern countries sent entire fleets

Germanicus's triumphal arch, Saintes.

Statue at Pons, on the pilgrim's route to Santiago de Compostela.

in search of this product, which could not be harvested in their climate, and which they desperately needed to preserve fish. For them, this stop was also an opportunity to add a few barrels of wine to their cargo, and so prolong the pleasure they had in discovering this new beverage in their own country. The area was also a way station on the pilgrims' route to Santiago de Compostela in Spain, along which the faithful erected churches and abbeys here and there, usually at major crossroads. So while William, the Norman duke, prepared to invade England in 1066 and to merit his epithet "the Conqueror," the Charentais winegrowers already had long years of trade behind them with Scots, Danish Vikings, and Andalusian Moors.

"Broom" and Bust

From 1120, under William X, duke of Aquitaine, count of Poitiers, and father of the famous Eleanor, it was the port of La Rochelle that grew into a trading town, while Bordeaux was only the administrative capital of the duchy. The beautiful Eleanor's first marriage, in 1137, to Louis VII, king of France, brought Charentais wines to Paris. The marriage was annulled in 1152, and she remarried the same year, this time to the count of Anjou, Henry II Plantagenet (which literally means, "sprig of broom," and was worn as a crest by the Plantagenets). He would become king of England, opening up an entire new country to the Charentais traders. When John Lackland ascended

Abbey in Chartres.

to the English throne, succeeding his brother, Richard Lion-Heart, he granted certain political and economic privileges to the town of Cognac*. These included assigning the name cognac—rather than that of the neighboring town of Jarnac*—to what was then only a fairly ordinary white wine, but which would soon attract attention under a more distilled form.

Ruins of a castle in Bouteville.

The year 1224 was an important one for Bordeaux, and the Gironde region around Bordeaux turned into a border area, as Angoumois, Saintonge, and Aunis—along with Angoulême, Cognac, and La Rochelle—became French again. De facto, Bordeaux, the capital of the Gironde, found itself opened to the English market, while Charentais wines were presented to the French court. Times of good and bad fortune followed. During the Hundred Years War, the English regularly devastated the vineyards bordering enemy territory, while Bordeaux's flourishing international maritime trade increased its wealth. On French soil, competition was fierce, and other vineyards closer to the capital—those of the Loire, of Burgundy, of the Aÿ in Champagne, and even of the Île de France regions around the capital (Suresne had the vines with the best reputation)—won the market, as their proximity provided a better value product. For an entire century, the Charente* region was forgotten. The vineyards were abandoned, and farmers raised grain where the land was fertile (the Petite* and Grande Champagne* production areas). Elsewhere, the land was

Entry to the port at La Rochelle.

Pot-still at a distillery in Charente.

forested, which would in time provide the names of the production areas Borderies*, or adjoining lands, and Bois*, woods. A few surviving vineyards provided for local consumption* and religious needs.

In 1475, Louis XI and Edward IV signed the Treaty of Picquigny, marking the end of the Hundred Years War. This year was full of hope; at the same time the king of France granted the vinegar-makers on the banks of the Charente River the right to "burn" their excess wine, giving an official seal to an age-old practice that until then had remained unauthorized. And fortunately so, because though these kings did not leave much of a mark in cognac's history, they thus perpetuated a secondary production method that would, a few centuries later, overtake that of the wine itself.

"Good King" Henry IV's Edict of Nantes brought an end to the Wars of Religion (1562–98), but the privileges accorded to the Huguenot capital of La Rochelle were not to the liking of Louis XIII. Richelieu rescinded them in 1628, after a siege lasting more than 400 days. The hunt for Protestants was on. The Charentais often offered asylum to fugitives, and this liberal attitude again allowed the region's products to reach major trade capitals in countries loyal to the Reform. Wine trade resumed with London, Amsterdam, Copenhagen, and even Hamburg, and vineyards, replanted in haste, took over the region, relegating grain to the rank of a secondary crop. Many Charentais people set out to make wine.

Good Times and Bad

Many turned quickly into too many. While the quality wines of the Petite* and Grande Champagne* found openings for export, transport to the coastal ports was overtaxed. The exasperation of the Angoumois winegrowers grew until it led to a peasant uprising in 1636 that history would remember under the name "Revolt of the Croquants." The little Aunis wines, which did not travel well, had an even harder time selling, even though they were closer to the shipping ports and therefore taxed less to reach their destination. Perhaps they were not of high enough quality, and wine drinkers at the time were becoming more demanding. Whatever the causes, the overall poor sales of Charentais wines would have a major impact on the region and its economy, one nobody at the time could have predicted. Unable to sell the wine they made (and some unable to do anything with it but make vinegar), the Charentais set out to "burn" it, as had the fifteenth-century vinegar-makers. That is, they distilled it into brandy. Other regions were already producing brandy; the town of Colmar had a distillation* inspector as early as 1506! Here, however, the process was at first nothing more than a last resort, implemented, some must have said, while awaiting more prosperous times. They carried out this operation at the risk of stripping the district of its forests since, in order to distill wine, one had to heat it beyond the temperature at which alcohol boils (173°F/78.3°C), which called for a massive use of wood.

The Saving Spirit

During the religious conflicts, the great navigating Dutch carried a kind of grain alcohol aboard their ships, until a few poor harvests led them to seek a substitute. They imported the little Aunis wines—which traveled so poorly—at low prices, and made brandwijn (burned wine), or brandy, with it. Then, due to the cost of transport, Batavian tradesmen chose to distill the wine prior to loading it, thus transporting a brandy whose volume was six to eight times smaller. The Charentais, who had already begun

The *Spirit of Hennessy*, heading East.

distilling their wine, improved their first pot-stills*, perfecting the process of doubling*, that is, the system of double distillation. This improved the quality of the alcohol, and it was discovered that not only could it be drunk pure but, most of all, when stored in oak* barrels for several years, it turned into pure nectar. The English, in 1678, enjoyed it under the name of brandy, then under the name of cognac, a spirit very different from others made in Bordeaux, Nantes, and even La Rochelle, as it was already subject to most of the rigorous criteria that account for the quality and uniqueness we know today.

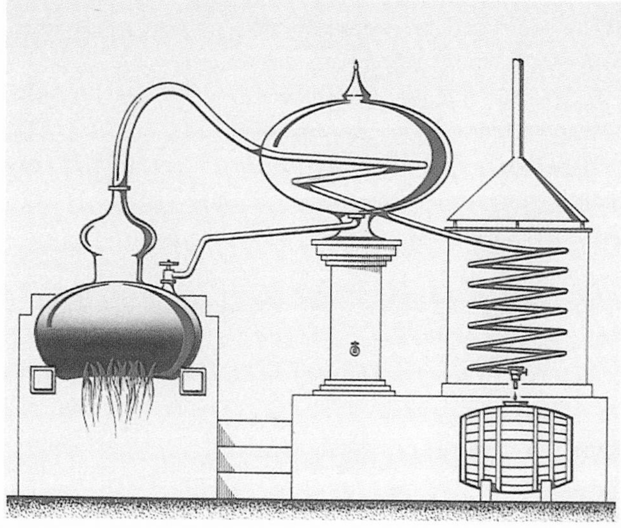

Diagram of a Charentais pot-still.

The process of distillation was one that had long been discussed. In his treatise on wine and spirits, the Catalan physician Arnáu de Vilanova, professor at the University of Montpellier until 1311, writes about aqua vitae as a "universal remedy*." It is said that he held the secrets of distillation from his studies in Moorish Spain, and in France he described the ancestor of the pot-still, or alembic (from the Arabic al-ambiq). Drawings exist of even older, more basic forms of stills.

King Louis XIV did not want to leave the monopoly on maritime trade to the Dutch, who were enemies of France at the time, so he decided to build a fleet, setting up the Rochefort shipyard and its celebrated rope-making industry at the mouth of the Charente* River. He also had oak forests planted in the regions of Tronçais and Limousin, while the Charente winemakers were cutting theirs down, replacing them with grapevines as in previous times, but this time to produce their famous cognac. This is the origin of the Bois* (woods) region. The two

Champagne* areas, Grande and Petite, were once again covered in vineyards. Although the product was experiencing rapid growth, conflicts involving various nations were creating obstacles to the European expansion of trade. Survival sometimes required transgression of the law, with spirits and contraband often finding their fates bound together. On land, fast horses attached to light carriages outwitted tax collectors, while at sea, small boats boldly, and precisely, passed under the noses of the coast guards.

Oak forest, which will be used to make casks.

The Channel Island of Jersey, across from the Normandy peninsula of Cotentin, became a hub for smugglers. One of its inhabitants, Jean Martell, moved to Cognac* in 1715 and founded a trading house that dealt in a range of products, including cognac, until that became the firm's mainstay. Some years later, in 1765, the Irish captain Richard Hennessy (after fifteen years at the service of Louis IV, fighting throughout Europe) also created his own trading post in Cognac, founding the establishment that still carries his name today. Subject to the vagaries of Franco-English relations, Richard and his son James had the brilliant idea of establishing a triangular trade route connecting the port of Cognac with the neutral port of Ostende in the Netherlands and with London, where another major name, George Sandeman, opened his company's doors to their exports.

The long building of the former royal rope-making factory in Rochefort.

Richard Hennessy, founder of the famous cognac firm.

Prosperity would limit the impact of the French Revolution. The bourgeoisie, driving through new ideas as much as revenging themselves on a declining nobility*, were not troubled; they understood their duty to maintain good relations with winemakers and distillers. Winegrowers, distillers, and merchants had nothing to complain about at the end of the Ancien Régime—Louis XVI had accorded a total exemption from export taxes on wine and alcohol in 1784 and, two years later, English entry duties were reduced. Even the harsh winter of 1788–89, whose very cold frosts damaged the vineyards, did not spawn an actual crisis, but rather strengthened the bonds of solidarity among farmers, winegrowers, and merchants.

If the name Napoleon* appears on bottles* of cognac today, it's because of Napoleon III, who was much more appreciated in the thatched cottages than was his uncle Napoleon Bonaparte. The Continental System trade blockade, and the nearly incessant state of war during Napoleon I's reign, led to the total interruption of all normal export activity, setting the stage for smuggling, which inevitably affected the profits of all the properly organized businesses. The Restoration returned prosperity to the region, where new trading houses began shipping their brandies in bottles rather than barrels, with signatures and brands protected by law in 1857. The Second Empire was cognac's golden age. Even if the labels sport the image of Napoleon Bonaparte, it was his nephew who conquered the heart, and bankbooks, of the Charentais, with the free-trade treaty signed with England, their best customer. The vineyards became the largest in France, extending to the offshore islands. Parts of Ré, Blanche, and Oléron islands were planted with cognac vines. At the same time, the cardboard industry developed, and printers, glass*-makers, and cork- and crate-makers found work. Exports, which were barely 924,700 gallons (35,000 hl) in 1815, grew to over 11 million gallons (420,000 hl) in 1860.

Loading a river barge on the wharves of the Charente River in Cognac.

Vastatrix, the Attack

In cognac country, the bad luck continued. Barely had the Second Empire collapsed when, in 1872, an invasion that had nothing Prussian about it struck the vineyard. Phylloxera* (*Phylloxera vastatrix*) upheld its Latin name and, perhaps here more than elsewhere, devastated the vineyards at a time when overproduction and large stocks* were already putting the treasuries under a strain. All those who did not have sufficient financial reserves ended up frenziedly unloading their stocks, while nearly 90 percent of the vineyards had to be uprooted. In these troubled times, the prestige of the word "cognac" attracted a number of crooks, who shamelessly usurped the name to unload brandies of all kinds that had no connection at all to the Charente* spirit.

But evil can bring good with it: when control returned it did so with a vengeance in a battle against fraud that would be the origin of one of the most draconian, and reassuring, set of regulations* in existence. Native American rootstock was imported for grafting, and once again the Charente region called on solidarity to relaunch the winemaking industry. In 1909, the name cognac was protected by a law, broadened in 1929 by the attribution of the "acquit* jaune d'or," a certificate guaranteeing place of origin. The law stipulates that cognac can only come from a delimited area, strictly regulates the denominations, and precisely defines the spirit's production and maturation processes. In 1938, the national

American rootstock: the conqueror of phylloxera.

Cognac vineyards throughout the seasons.

AOC (*Appellation d'Origine Contrôlée*) registered labeling system modified the areas of production territories, benifiting some and not others; agreement was reached without major disagreement.

During the Second World War, foreign occupation threatened the region's economy. Poor sales once again bloated the stocks, which the Charentais feared they would have to turn over as booty to the Germans. At this time, the industry's first professional organization, the Bureau de Répartition des Vins et Eaux-de-Vie, was founded; at the Liberation it became the Bureau National Interprofessionnel du Cognac (BNIC*), which is the name by which it is still known today.

Modern Times

The twentieth century was marked by the reconstitution of the vineyards, which today cover 197,682 acres (80,000 ha), far less than the surface area covered prior to phylloxera*.

Until hard times hit at the beginning of the 1970s, the volume of sales increased regularly (as did stocks*, for that matter), allowing a certain number of major firms not only to gain worldwide recognition, but even to be integrated into multinational luxury goods corporations. Major financial changes overthrew the established hierarchies, and small producers had to change their strategies in order to survive. Some of them—though they were in the minority—tried marketing their product under their own name. In so doing, they contribute to the diversity and renewal of flavors that constitute quality regional products. Similarly, major firms contribute to sustaining the quality, balance, and harmony of the prestigious blends, ensuring that a fine cognac will never disappoint, and will always stand out throughout the world.

Maurice Chevalier as a cognac ambassador in Ernst Lubitsch's *A Smiling Lieutenant* (1932).

HENNESSY

Acquit

When a spirit travels, it has to pay, just like a person does. The authorities responsible for indirect taxation, who are mobile and carry out impromptu checks, often at night, have always been there to collect and/or control the taxes paid to the state.

"Your papers, please!" This order goes for people driving their cars, just as it does for traveling spirits. And when it comes to papers, spirits have their fair share. There are no traceability problems here. Right from its birth in the distillery, the brandy is recorded in the appropriate registry. Then, with each passing year, the *compte d'âge* age index* record keeps track of it. When it reaches thirty months, it is allowed to travel.

When the duty taxes on wine have been paid and then reflected in the sales price (as is the case with all bottles* bought by individuals), a clearance, which in France takes the form of a seal with an image of the national Marianne symbol, appears on the top of the bottle cap surrounded by a color. This measure also applies to spirits, and therefore to cognac.

If transport occurs prior to its definitive sale, the situation is different. As the duties have not yet been paid, the authorities deliver a special paper containing all shipping details (location, itinerary, quantity, packaging, schedule). Over the years, and after different decrees, this certificate changed color: it was red in 1872, then white in 1903, turning to golden yellow (*jaune d'or*) on August 4, 1929. This final decree may not have abolished certain privileges, but it did make fraud much more difficult by perfecting the "*acquit jaune d'or,*" or golden-yellow receipt, making it both a simpler and more complete certificate of origin. Today, it has been replaced by the Community Accompanying Document.

A Charentais pot-still.

Age Index (Compte d'Âge)

The distillation* period begins just as the fermentation of the wine ends, and must, without fail, be completed by March 31 of the next year. The vintage* produced during this period of time is recorded with the regulatory agency under what is called *compte* 00. The following

Recording the age of the spirits.

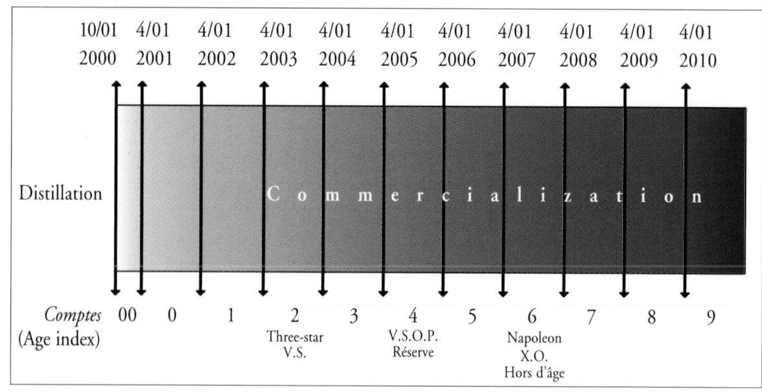

year, on April 1, this same vintage will be referenced as *compte* 0, and the following year on the anniversary date, as *compte* 1.

It can only be marketed one year later, when it is at *compte* 2—that is, when the cognac is in its third year. In reality, it waits longer, increasing in *comptes*, before it leaves the stocks*. From *compte* 2, the young brandy will be used in the blending* of cognacs with V.S. and Three-star designations.

The V.O. and V.S.O.P. cognacs must not include cognacs younger than *compte* 4.

"Paradise": the reserve for the oldest cognacs in the *chai*.

Cognacs bearing Napoleon*, X.O., Hors d'Âge, or other similar accepted designations, contain no brandy younger than *compte* 6. The final classification is *compte* 9, which applies to all older brandies.

Aging in casks can last a very long time.

Aging

Legend has it that toward 1620, casks "forgotten" for several years on a wharf—others say it was a barrel lost in the depths of a knight's cellar—were discovered to contain a Cognac brandy that had improved over the time it had been forgotten in oak*, revealing flavors and aromas* that the usual near-immediate consumption* of the spirit had never uncovered.

For easily understandable financial reasons, the spirit was marketed as quickly as possible after it was produced. It would never have crossed the mind of any "real" Charentais to store it. But this chance discovery would revolutionize the trade. If the brandy could be kept, stocks* would allow for the regulation* of the market, both in quantity—for the years of smaller harvests—and in quality—for those of mediocre harvests. It would no longer be enough to simply produce in order to sell, but one would have to store the brandy in order to age it. And since the product improved and acquired added value when aged, the Charentais understood that they would be able to sell it at a higher price. As people with a healthy respect for profit, but who also like a job well done, they took advantage of this new approach to improve the quality, making skillful blends by marrying their different outputs according to complex, and secret, rules.

Only recently have the virtues of the wooden barrel been understood. At the beginning of the nineteenth century,

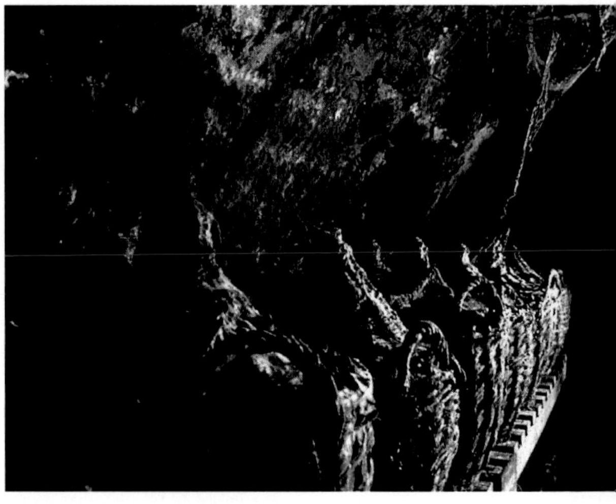

After maturing in a cask, the cognac goes into demijohns.

The angels' share rises heavenward in the darkness of the *chais*.

Jean-Antoine Chaptal, the French chemist who contributed much to industrialization, did not show much enthusiasm for casks. He decried the variations in their capacity, calling for a reform of weights and measures that was slow in coming (and actually would never occur in cooperage*). However, it was finally understand how the pores of the oak* from the Limousin forests, used to make casks, played a role in the interaction of the brandy with oxygen found in the air. It was realized that this interplay, by reducing the alcohol content, was the basis of the aging process and of the product's improvement over time. In this way, the producers were more easily able to accept the notion of the "angels' share*"—the 2 to 3 percent annual evaporation inherent to the process. It also explained the characteristic dark shade of the storehouse façades, which darken due to a microscopic fungus, *Torula compniacencis*, which feeds on the alcohol vapors.

■ Angels' Share

Every day, alcohol vapors escape from the casks stored in the *chais**, evaporating into the air. As children and poets have explained, if they do so, it is because they have wings and, as we cannot see them, these vapors end up as the angels' share, belonging to those happy beings who are not content simply to watch over us from the heavens. This may also help to explain much of the disorder found on this earth. This share is far from negligible: it represents some 27 million bottles* a year, or three-and-a-half times the entire French consumption* of cognac. You might well ask yourself if the angels are still flying straight!

Even if this evaporation could be impeded it would not be, as it is indispensable to the aging* of the cognac, despite lightening the stocks by 2 to 3 percent and blackening the walls of the storehouses. The more the latter are ventilated, the more the air of Cognac*, Jarnac*, and other places where this divine elixir lies, is filled with quite curious fragrances capable of making you give in to temptation. It would be unfair for your guardian angel to reproach you. Nevertheless, the angels' share is expensive, as it becomes necessary to fill the empty space left each year by evaporation with either an identical brandy, or one of a different age and origin. This operation provides the cellar master* with an opportunity to adjust his blend depending on the cognac's evolution.

Aromas

What could be subtler to explain and describe than aromas? According to the dictionary, they are "...the distinctive fragrance of a spice, plant, etc., an agreeable odor, a distinctive, pervasive, and usually pleasant or savory smell." In reference to cognac, however, the term has a very specific meaning. You speak of aromas during the olfactory tasting*. The word does not refer to the most volatile initial impressions you smell on first contact, the first nose, but to the second nose, which provides the broad range of fragrances that make up the actual aroma. The combination of both first nose and second nose constitutes the bouquet.

You also encounter aromas during the gustatory study, when, allied with the savor (the sensation experienced by the tongue and the palate), they form the taste (all the sensations experienced by the mouth). Primary aromas refer to the first gustatory sensations that generally evoke fruit and sometimes flowers. Secondary aromas are those resulting from the distillation* process. Tertiary aromas cover the woody impressions that appear afterwards, often identified as toasty, spicy, or smoky, and which come primarily from the oak* of the barrels, by way of complex interactions that occur between the wood and the spirit.

Old-time cellar master appraising aromas to prepare his blend.

The river barges had a collapsible mast so that they could go under bridges.

Barge

Although it was never very deep, the Charente* River used to be navigable and served as the main transport route for salt coming inland from the coast. The barges that transported the salt were called *gabares*, perhaps after the famous gabelle, the tax levied on salt prior to 1790.

Although the river was relatively navigable, it required a boat without much draft, and therefore preferably with a flat bottom, but nevertheless capable of taking on significant amounts of cargo. As it had to be hauled upstream, it also had to be light, and equipped with a collapsible mast in order to pass under bridges, and with a sail to go down-river. These barges were seen on the Charente River well after the birth of steamboats.

At the town of Tonnay-Charente, the barges were loaded with salt, wheat, and furs imported from Northern Europe and Canada. They moved upstream at the pace of the cattle that hauled them by way of Saintes, Cognac*, and Jarnac*, river ports where the salt was often traded for casks of wine or brandy destined to remain in France or travel abroad. When they arrived at Angoulême, they loaded carving stones from the nearby quarries or beams of oak* from the Limousin forests, or sometimes gunpowder and cannons for arming the ships at the Rochefort shipyards. They then floated down-river, calling at the ports they stopped at on the way up, picking up barrels and crates destined for export by the ships waiting at Tonnay-Charente or La Rochelle.

The barges provided slow but reliable, practical, and inexpensive transport that avoided the chaos of roads in poor condition. It suited the easygoing mentality of the Charentais very well, and justifies the nickname often given to the residents of Angoumois in the local dialect—*cagouillard* or *cagouille*, meaning snail. Could the tranquility and stately slowness of the river have something to do with this?

Batches

Known as *manches* in French, these are the brandies selected as soon as they leave the still for gustatory qualities that are traditional, or characteristic of their provenance. Controlled, they are grouped in distinct batches based on their nuances: floral, fruity, woody, or spicy. They serve as a basis for the first blends following the instructions set down in the house blending* pattern.

Blending

The large majority of cognacs sold in bottles* are, in fact, mixtures of several brandies. They may be made using a combination of different *crus**, different grape varieties*, or different distillation* methods, just as they may contain some vintage* brandy or one from a cask with some specific characteristics. The complex and delicate process of blending is based on factors so varied that you could almost add the age of the cellar master* to the list of criteria.

In fact, the aim is simple: to use different products in order to produce characteristics and a flavor that do not change for the customer, so that the cognac is consistent in character* and taste and to ensure that the customer remains loyal to his preferred brand.
In order to do this, the cellar master has at his disposal a whole range of possibilities. He must remember previous blends, taking into consideration nuances that could have affected them. His memory must not only be cerebral, but olfactory,

A cellar master examining samples.

Blending vats.

visual, and gustatory. The major cognac firms use a blend pattern, rather like a dress-making pattern, which serves as a kind of model and is kept secret, of course. It outlines the cognac's composition, specifying references and proportions that are updated every year.

The brandies are grouped together in batches* based on very precise quality standards and flavor nuances: woody, floral, fruity, spicy. The cellar master has at hand, or rather at nose, all the elements necessary to compose the first blend based on the pattern.

This document, a written memory, provides a kind of guide to finding the specific aromas* of the reference vintage, based on the elements previously used to arrive at that blend. The major difficulty comes from the fact that the elements available now are necessarily different from yesterday's elements, and their evolution is far from being of a reliable consistency. This first cut *could be set aside to age in an oak* cask. The choice depends solely on the cellar master's decision, which is based on the results of his tasting. He could also modify some proportions, taking the time to determine how this "pre-nuptial agreement" is coming along, before deciding to complete the blending.

After the necessary months or years, punctuated by regular tastings, the cellar master finally decides on the "marriage." This is the final cut, which will have the privilege of aging in an oak barrel, calmly waiting the decision to bottle.

To be successful, blending requires a cellar master with long years of experience, and he or she is the keystone of a brand's success. There are few people capable of performing this highly specialized role.

Cupboard for storing cognac samples.

BNIC

As with all the wine-related industries in France, for about a century the winegrowers and traders of the Cognac region have combined their efforts by uniting together under the aegis of a single professional organization. After the Second World War, they established the Bureau National Interprofessionnel du Cognac (BNIC), heir to the Bureau de Repartition des Vins et Eaux-de-Vie. These two institutions demonstrate the constant desire of the Charentais to resolve peaceably any difficulties that may arise within the industry. All major issues in the region—reforms concerning vineyard structure, division of production areas, specification of production methods—have been resolved without any major storms, from the time of the official recognition of cognac in 1909 through to the definition of the *acquit* jaune d'or* in 1929, the linking to the AOC system in 1938, and the delimitation and attribution of the various production areas. The BNIC groups together cognac professionals who jointly define all the programs aimed at protecting and promoting the quality and reputation of the product.

A private establishment with a public-service mission, the BNIC is jointly financed by professionals in the cognac industry with the goal of defending the interests of all those who participate in its economy. It controls the movement of cognac, verifies the age index*, and ensures the delivery of age and origin certificates, with the help of a state-appointed inspector who is nominated by the finance minister and the heads of the different administrations involved. The BNIC is also involved in scientific research, statistical analysis, communication, research, and the monitoring of worldwide legislation related to winegrowing aid and the fight against fraud.

Headquarters of the BNIC in Cognac.

Forests are still present throughout the Charente. They gave their name to several cognac production areas.

Bois

The names of three minor cognac *crus**, or production areas, serve as reminders that before being planted with grapevines, the region was covered with trees, forming the woods or *bois* that today still separate the vineyard areas.

The Fins Bois, with 77,970 acres (31,554 ha.) of cognac grapevines, forms the largest entity of the winegrowing region. The soil, while still chalky, is mixed with clay and sand, and enriched by a thick layer of humus left by the forests that still covered the region in the fourteenth century. The brandies from the Fins Bois, although they do not have the finesse and elegance of those from the Champagne* zones, do have strength and body, and

Map of Fins Bois.

mature relatively quickly. In the Bons Bois soil, chalk gives way to clay, and is only found in islets under a lighter forest humus. The western part of the area is already exposed to maritime influences. The brandies made from these 26,730 acres (10,817 ha.) of grapevines have a strong earthy quality. Aging* rather quickly, they make effective elements for cognac blending*, as long as one is not afraid of novelty or originality.

The Bois Ordinaires are sometimes called "Communs" or *à terroir*, and accommodate themselves to their adjective of "ordinary." Burgundy wine also has its "ordinary" wines, known as Grand Ordinaire, which are, it is true, embellished with the word "grand," as if it were necessary to compensate for the initial qualifier. In any case, it is this "ordinary" that, by serving as a reference (which is important in itself), allows for the full appreciation of the quality scale, right through to those exceptional cognacs. The Bois Ordinaires produce cognacs that some would say have only one quality—their price. They are certainly not Fine* Champagne, but perhaps at a café counter in France you will discover the qualities of these Bois Ordinaires. With a little attention—and imagination—you can discover in them a slight fragrance of iodine, of kelp, and an ocean breeze, without losing the pronounced earthy flavors linked to the land. This is the charm of these coastal and island cognacs.

Borderies

This production area corresponds to the zone that formerly marked the limit between fields and woods. It is

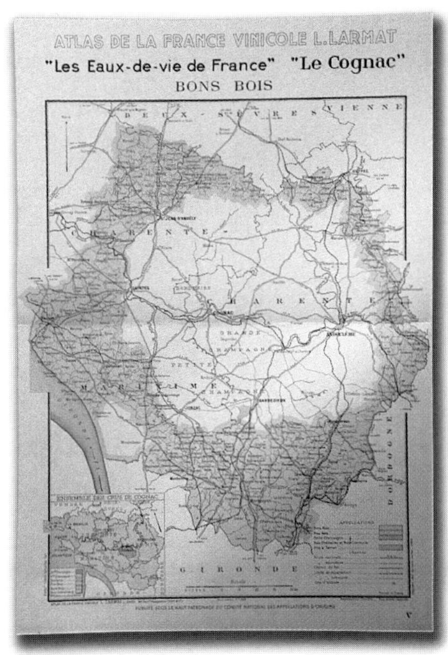

Map of Bons Bois.

Map of Borderies and Petite Champagne.

the smallest cognac *cru** with only 9640 acres (3901 ha.) of vineyards planted in a soil whose half-decomposed chalk began to incorporate clay and flint when the Charente* River valley formed in the Tertiary period. The brandies produced here are sought after for their ability to age quickly, while maintaining a character and softness much appreciated for tasting* and for incorporating into quality blends.

Bottle

When glass bottles replaced oak* barrels for transporting cognac, a new commercial strategy was born. Unlike wine, spirits do not continue to mature once they have been bottled. In fact, they may even

Traditional cognac bottle.

Contemporary cognac bottle.

evaporate if poorly sealed. Packaging in glass seems to date from the eighteenth century, first in demijohns, those large potbellied bottles that are often wrapped in wicker for better protection. They facilitated transport and export, but most of all they guaranteed the quality obtained by the cellar master* in Charente*. From there, it

Engraved crystal carafe.

Contemporary cognac container inspired by perfume bottles.

Old bottle of a Grande Champagage Emperor's Reserve cognac.

was a short step to move on to a smaller bottle, although this change did not occur immediately. Individual bottling only began at the beginning of the nineteenth century, and for a long time it was reserved exclusively for the most prestigious customers of major cognac producers. In the middle of the century, individual bottles became a selling point in themselves, guaranteeing authenticity and strengthening brand names. For yet another century, presentation was limited to traditional bottles that were all uniform no matter what the quality of the beverage they contained. Shipping in barrels (which now only has symbolic value) practically came to an end in the 1910s.

Each bottle or transparent 23.33 fl oz (70 cl) container reveals the golden amber of the Charentais treasure. It also adds to the effect of the brand name found on the label. This new container quickly became a means of competing with other vineyards, with each producer seeking a strong visual identifier linked to its name, one defining the brand at first glance—whether it was a famous effigy with a cocked hat, the arm of a medieval knight bearing an ax, an imperial eagle, or coats of arms. Commercial logos are nothing new.

If the traditional cylindrical bottle, often associated with Bordeaux wines, has the merit of being classic in design, the possibilities presented by creating various other shapes of bottle did not escape the attention of some producers, often with the complicity of glassmakers. They made, and continue to make, veritable masterpieces worthy of this beverage's mastered art. In a variation on poet Alfred de Musset's famous expression, "Never mind the bottle, as long as you have drunkenness," here you could say, "Never mind the drunkenness, as long as you have the bottle." As for ordinary containers in everyday glass*, in the 1890s it became easier and more economical to make them with the invention of a bottle-making machine (so no more glassblowing), perfected by Claude Boucher (1842–1913), a glassmaker in Cognac*.

Brouillis

Contrary to what is frequently thought, cognac does not result from a distillation* of pineau*, nor is it actually made from a "finished" new wine. What is distilled is in fact a fermented grape-must, or, if you prefer, an unfiltered wine, which is boiled in the pot-still* and condensed by refrigeration. Then, from the copper coil, comes a slightly cloudy liquid with an alcohol content of about 27 to 30 percent by volume that is called the *brouillis.* This liquid will then be distilled again to make the cognac.

Calligraphy

In the darkness of the cellars, on the bilge (the central, widest part of the barrel) of the first casks heading the lines of barrels, you can read initials, names, and dates, all written in chalk. What is surprising is the care with which these words are written, using a calligraphy that, with its full lines and tapering strokes, recalls the finesse and strength of ancient writing styles, with their evocative names such as "roundhand" or "Gothic." This detail, part of a long tradition of perfection, expresses a true artist's talent.

Cellar Master

The envied title of master has always inspired deference and respect. The very meaning of the word implies a recognition of superiority. The domains of art, education, law, crafts, and music give titles to their elite. In winemaking, it goes to the master of the *chai**, or the cellar. Who is this cellar master and what is his role? First of all, he is someone with experience, who necessarily comes from the world of cognac. He has an in-depth knowledge of every aspect of cognac-making, from the soil under the vines to the climate* above them, and has for bedside-reading the archives of the firm he works for. His memory must be good enough to remember that, perhaps well before his time, a certain blend reached the sought-after goal one year and not another. He has to know how a brandy evolved when it came from a particular plot of land, under given climatic conditions, from the time of the vine's flowering through to aging* in casks in

Yann Fillioux, cellar master for the Hennessy firm.

Maurice Hennessy, the brand's ambassador.

the *chai*. But the cellar master is a powerful man who must also be decisive. He may take the time to consult his assistants, to talk to his winegrowers, to speak with his coopers about the wood used for casks, yet he never neglects his responsibilities, and always assumes them fully when it is a question of making a decision on blending*. His employers have total trust in him, a trust that can be measured by the amounts of money at stake. The person with the final responsibility for the sales (the dealer) and the one who has the final responsibility for the production (the blender) —that is, the cellar master and therefore the master blender—have to work very closely with one another.

The strength of this two-way relationship is illustrated by the seven generations of cellar masters from the Fillioux family who have worked at Hennessy since 1800, an ongoing partnership that is over two centuries old. This profession* cannot be learned in books, nor entirely at school. A cellar master learns from his father, his nose steeped in cognac from childhood. Following his father to work, pre-trained on the job, he is invited to breathe in the odors, to smell the aromas*, at an age when others are licking lollipops.

CHAI

Today winegrowers all over France use the word *chai* to designate the place where they store the wine and spirit barrels during the maturation and aging* phases. However, the Charente* district could rightly claim, if not its exclusive use, at least the paternity of this word. According to the dictionary (which, of course, like a good spirit, cannot go wrong), *chai* is the regional form of the word *quai*, meaning wharf or quay, which in turn comes from the Gallic word *caio*. It is therefore not astonishing that the *chais* in Cognac are never underground, but rather always at ground level, often on the banks of the Charente River—on the wharves, to be precise. Variations in temperature are apparently favorable to the aging and maturation of this spirit.

The oldest cognacs are found under lock and key, well protected in a special corner of the storage area, accessible only to a privileged few when duly accompanied by the cellar master*. This sanctum is called the "paradise," evidently placed under the protection of the highest of angels.

Above: Casks and, behind, demijohns, a small corner of "paradise."

Chalk inscriptions (left) identify very old spirits used in prestigious blends.

Facing page: Casks stacked in the storehouses of a major cognac firm.

A cross-section of the soil in Grande Champagne showing its fine, chalky composition.

Champagne

Not to be confused with France's great sparkling wine, the "*champagne*" we are interested in here refers to the fields or *champs*, cleared over the centuries, which surround a certain number of villages and towns, of which Cognac* is the central point. *Champagne* is an archaic form of "*campagne,*" the French word for countryside, and is employed to distinguish the land it describes from the surrounding woods. Logically, the Borderies*, or adjoining lands, can be found on the edges of the two Champagne *crus**; the whole is surrounded by the Bois*, or woods, which are classed by decreasing order starting from their proximity to the town of Cognac—Fins, Bons, and Ordinaires. There is a certain similarity between the soil found in the central Charente* region and that found in the Champagne region, where the sparkling wine is produced. All similarities between the two regions end there, as grape varieties* and final products differ. This soil type is not found exclusively in these two regions of France, *champagne* being a more general geological term for a chalky plain, rich in limestone.

Character

All farmers are attached to their land, but Charentais winegrowers are attached to it by the very roots of their grapevines. Contrary to what many city dwellers might think, this anchorage (and some of these farmers are also sailors) is that much stronger the harder the work. Like all harvests, the crop cannot wait, and nothing can be put before it. This necessary priority has taught the winegrower to depend only on himself (or his family or clan). His individualism is therefore not surprising, and it only finds exception in the relationships he can cultivate with his colleagues.

In the Charente* region, this character trait manifests itself in the dwellings. The farms, enclosed by high walls with a double gate that is rarely open (except through forgetfulness), seem to isolate themselves among the vineyards. A water* source often determined where vines would be planted, leading to the founding of a farm or a hamlet. The "Maine," related to such words as manse, manor, and mansion, is found in such place names as Maine-Giraud or Maine-Allard, for example, and originally designated a hamlet inhabited by the extended family—an actual clan—of the Girauds or the Allards.

Even when grouped together in villages, the farms had the same layout—almost windowless high walls line the streets, with only the gates breaking up this chosen alignment of blind façades. But if you manage to find your way inside, the welcome is warm. You will discover a well-lit, spacious, and comfortable home, whose

A typical Charentais enclosed farm.

inhabitants are well informed, up-to-date, and more aware of world problems than you might have imagined, right in line with the questing commercial spirit they inherited from their bold ancestors. As early as the Middle Ages, the Charentais embraced a horizon broader than the lord's land and castle. The sea and salt opened them to trade. With these resources, not to say this wealth, came the drawback of being coveted and then torn apart by France and England. Although the Charentais suffered in some ways, they also gained a certain independence, which was illustrated in the way they built up foreign trade relations that were sometimes far from orthodox—and occasionally seemed closer to smuggling than to the national policies set in the capital.

Merchant more than soldier, any sensible Charentais detests war, which he knows will ruin trade. He can be placid and philosophical, just as he has been known to revolt against any unjust taxation that might bring shortages or impinge on his prosperity. He has also been known to join uprisings and revolts to defend his faith and convictions.

But even today, what attaches him most to the land is his cognac. He knows he has one of the most beautiful occupations in the world, because he produces the very best spirit found on this earth. Who could blame him for his pride? This man applies his will to the raising of his grapevine, his know-how to vinification*, his inspiration to his glorious blends, and his patience to the aging* process.

And what does he dream about, when he is exhausted, dropping from fatigue, in the middle of winter, sleeping next to his furnace and his pot-still* like a father watching over a child? Perhaps of a paradise where the angels would not take their share of his labor, leaving his cognac to age in peace for eternity, and thus accomplish the miracle of the ultimate aromas* of a universal spirit that would, of course, be divine.

Charente

In the singular form, Charente is a tranquil river only 224 miles (360 km) long, which starts in the Limousin region and gently flows to the Atlantic Ocean, by way of a wide, silty estuary. King Henry IV liked to say, "It's the most beautiful brook in my kingdom." On its way, it waters the town of Angoulême, known today for its comic-strip festival; the rival towns of Jarnac* and Cognac*; Saintes, the historic capital of Saintonge; Tonnay-Charente, the former river port where, at the beginning of the twentieth century, it was still possible to see barges* docking on one side and steamers on the other, and where salt, wine, and cognac were exported by sea; and finally Rochefort, with the long buildings of its former royal rope-making factory and its shipyards, where lovers of old-time sailing rigs set out to reconstruct the *Hermione*, the frigate that carried Lafayette to America in 1780.

When the word is used in the plural form, it refers to two departments, or French administrative districts, which since the Revolution have roughly covered the region that produces cognac, a spirit that can also use the old appellations *eau-de-vie des Charentes* and *eau-de-vie de Cognac*. The Charentes correspond to the territory covered by the three former provinces of Aunis, Saintonge, and Angoumois.

Again in the singular form, the Charente is the department that has Angoulême as capital and Cognac the sub-prefecture.

The other Charente department, Charente-Maritime, changed its name to *maritime* after being called *inférieure*, or secondary, for a long time. Its capital is the

The tranquil Charente River.

famous port of La Rochelle, and its sub-prefectures are all linked to the history of cognac: Rochefort, Saintes, Saint-Jean-d'Angély—three old river ports—and Jonzac, where hot springs and brandy combine to please everyone.
The Charentes are also, with the nearby Deux-Sèvres region, a dairy region, and so producers of another beverage—non-alcoholic this time—from which one of the best butters in France is made.

Heating unit of a traditional pot-still.

Chauffe

Distillation* depends on the heating, or *chauffe*, of a vat of wine—which, in the case of cognac, is actually fermented grape-must. Producing cognac requires a double distillation (doubling*), so a double heating, the first producing the *brouillis*, which has a low alcohol content, and the second being called the *bonne chauffe*. For each distillation, the first distilled liquid, the headings, and the last, the tailings, are eliminated, leaving only the "heart" that will become cognac. Until the end of the eighteenth century (and even quite some time afterward in the countryside), wood was used, as it was inexpensive and easy to get. However, it did not provide consistent heat, creating variations in temperature unacceptable in a process that requires constancy and regularity. In his famous 1801 essay on grape-based alcohol production, "*Traité de la Vigne, avec l'Art de Faire le Vin, les Eaux-de-Vie, Esprit de Vin, Vinaigres, et Composés*" ("Treaty on the Vine, With the Art of Making Wine, Eaux-de-Vie, Wine Spirit, Vinegar, and Composites"), French chemist and industrialist Jean-Antoine Chaptal wrote that a merchant from the town of Sète was the first to heat with coal, which was less expensive, easier to store, and offered a more consistent heat source, as the furnace needed loading less often. In turn, during the twentieth century, coal was replaced by gas, which is cheaper and more efficient and is still used today.

Vineyards in spring.

Climate

The delimited region with the right to use the cognac appellation is located some 62 miles (100 km) south of the Loire River, which gives it gentle weather with prevailing winds from the sea. Yet, when these are replaced by easterlies coming over the Auvergne mountains, the climate becomes nearly continental, sweeping the vineyard with cold wind and the threat of frost. Here, as elsewhere, hail also haunts winegrowers.

If bypassed by these two scourges, the Charentes* grapes can mature tranquilly, receiving attentive care from winemakers focused on producing a perfect final product. In the two Champagne* production areas, soil absorbs the sunshine, the chalk storing up the heat. In the Bois* and western areas, where the soil contains less chalk, ocean air dominates, with more humidity coming in the form of frequent mists and, sometimes, thick fog. These conditions do not keep the grapes from ripening, because the sun's ultraviolet rays continue to have an effect. The exceptional

light is sometimes blinding, but has the gift of softening the horizon with haze, its luminosity perhaps coming from a reflection off the ocean on one hand, and the Charente and Gironde Rivers on the other. It must be this light you see reflected in the color* of cognac.

Vineyards in summer (*above*) and in winter (*below*).

Cognac, the Town

The site of the present-day town of Cognac had everything to attract settlement—a large river, a little knoll, light but fertile soil, and surrounding woods.

The prehistoric inhabitants of Cognac were right to settle here; the village grew into a small town and then a larger town and experienced several thousand years of prosperity, marred by only a few misfortunes. The Benedictines also built a priory here, although they saved their spirit production for the town of Fécamp, where they created their eponymous liqueur, Benedictine.

As early as the eleventh century, the salt trade brought recognition to the port. Transported along the Charente* River from the coast, the salt was unloaded here then dispatched to its various destinations. Wine, from the vines the Romans had authorized, was also loaded on the boats, and when the Charentais "white gold" faced competition from less expensive Portuguese salt, the wharves in Cognac were lined with casks destined for the Dutch ships that were anchored off the coast. Such prosperity necessarily whetted appetites. Due to the different alliances and inheritances of the governing princes, for a time the inhabitants of Cognac became English. This did not necessarily displease them, as they were accorded various duty exemptions and privileges by John Lackland (1167–1216), brother of Richard Lion-Heart and also benefactor of the Saint-Émilion region in Bordeaux (whose vine stock found favorable soil in the Charente).

Flowing by Cognac, the Charente River was not always a tranquil river, and the city became used to power struggles. Even if it didn't experience a full century of conflict, it did become involved in the Hundred Years Wars, only becoming French again thanks to Connétable and Jean de Berry.

Sparing no effort, the inhabitants

River barges berthed at the wharves in Cognac, waiting to be loaded in front of the Hennessy warehouses at the beginning of the twentieth century.

The Pont-Neuf bridge over the Charente River and, to the right, the towers of the Saint-Jacques Gate, Cognac.

of Cognac revived the vineyards and returned to the trade of salt and wine. They again experienced prosperity under Charles d'Angoulême, who established a princely court at the Cognac castle to welcome poets—including Clément Marot—and artists. It was here that the future French Renaissance king, François I, was born in 1494. His castle has been the headquarters of the cognac firm Otard since 1796.

Embracing the Reform, Cognac would not be spared the torments of the Wars of Religion. This time loyal to the king of France during the Fronde revolts against the monarchy, Louis XIV rewarded the city with substantial privileges, notably in commerce (four trade fairs per year are authorized). The inhabitants of Cognac were also exempt from taxation for 20 years.

The seventeenth century was a turning point for the region. Perhaps too complacent, the Charentais were producing wines of poor quality that did not travel well. Poor sales, overproduction, transformation of stocks* into vinegar, and burning seemed to signal an end to prosperity...until the miraculous discovery, by chance, of a forgotten spirit, left in oak* barrels and improved beyond measure. Better placed than any other town to take advantage of the situation, Cognac was ready for revival. In the eighteenth

century, what we would now call an economic boom took Cognac—and the spirit that bore its name—to the forefront both in France and abroad, where this brandy was being snatched up. It seemed that nothing could stop its rise, which was given a further boost at the end of the nineteenth century by the introduction of bottling, until a nasty American vine louse, phylloxera*, arrived. Phylloxera would lay waste to all the French vineyards.
During its rise, all the major Franco-British trade names set themselves up in Cognac to try and make their fortune: Martell, Hennessy, Otard, and Delamain have since become world-renowned brands, ambassadors of French prestige abroad. At the same time, Cognac attracted hundreds of firms directly and indirectly linked to the spirit (packaging, shipping, etc.). This prosperity affected all the town's inhabitants, providing them with much better services and infrastructure than can be found in other towns of this size.
After another period of disarray, Cognac finally regained control. Today, the Bureau National Interprofessionnel du Cognac (BNIC*) has its home here, along with other organizations that govern the profession*. And the entire world welcomes Cognac's ambassadors, these representatives of the major firms, whose not quite diplomatic pouches often contain a very precious liquid.

Colombard, an authorized secondary grape variety.

Colombard

When the vineyards of the Charente* region still only produced wine—a sweet wine appreciated in England and northern Europe—they were primarily planted with Colombard (or Colombaud), a white grape variety*. This grape can be found throughout the Provence region; it adapts well to the hot, sometimes even torrid, summers that make beachgoing tourists happy in the nearby resort town of Royan and the islands of Ré and Oléron. It was probably the wine made from this Colombard variety that, as early as the twelfth century, accounted for the reputation of what were then called the Poitou vineyards. The French and English would fight over them long before and also after the Hundred Years War. Today, Colombard represents barely 10 percent of the Charentais vine stock.

The changing color of cognac over time.

Color

In the middle of winter, in the steamy heat of the Charentais distillery, cognac leaves the pot-still* as a transparent liquid. It measures 70 percent alcohol by volume. The distiller then places it in a brand-new oak* cask. The young spirit and the young wood interact, the latter soaking up the spirit, and the brandy begins to turn a pale yellow. This interchange with the wood will last a minimum of three years. After that time, the spirit has lost only a little of its strength, and still measures 65 percent alcohol by volume, although it has now taken on a beautiful golden color. Its barrel is changed to an auburn-colored used cask, which has given off its first tannins to another brandy. Our spirit is still young and hotheaded. Taken again at ten years, and still at 59 percent alcohol by volume, this brandy will have become a handsome little cognac. Its golden color has aged and is slightly amber from the slow oxidation of secondary tannins, the ones found deepest in the heart of the oak. Smooth and round, it melts in the mouth.

Fifteen is a fine age, with the cognac now at 55 percent by volume. The color is amber, with brown reflections. In the nose and mouth, something new appears: rancio*.

At twenty-five, and despite a major reduction* in volume (the angels* have taken their share—half the cask), our Grande Fine Champagne* still measures 50 percent by volume. Its color is mahogany with tawny nuances.

After half a century, it is still at 42 percent by volume. This is a venerable cognac, its deep color that of very old gold, with red flame reflections when struck by light. Tears and legs drape the sides of the glass*, signs of a viscosity that comes from the alcohol and glycerol, proof of its advanced age. It has a glorious nose.

Our spirit will continue to bear its color and aromas* in a bottle* or a demijohn, crossing the centuries, if the temptation to enjoy it does not become too strong.

CONSUMPTION

Is it treason against the king of spirits to talk about consumption? Is the word too vulgar for a brandy that considers itself to belong to an actual nobility of spirits with origins that are—and this is nearly a historical reality—more aristocratic than popular? We know the part ritual plays in the tasting* of a fine cognac—and are there any that are not fine? This is a product that results from the magic of blending*, a know-how that lies more in the realm of art than in commercial production. However, one cannot deny—particularly if one is from the Charentes* region—that cognac is a commercial product, ruled by the market, whose fluctuations are not without repercussions on the local economy.
Cognac is primarily distributed by dealers who generally do not own the vines; direct sales and those of cooperatives account for no more than 0.5 percent of total sales. The cognac that ends up in your glass*, whether at home, in a restaurant or a café, is almost always a "brand-name" cognac, the brand having participated, to varying degrees, in its distillation*, blending, aging*, bottling, and, of course, marketing.

Cognac with tonic, on the rocks.

A spirit made originally for export, cognac remains the most well-known and appreciated French spirit abroad. Its preferred market outside Europe (70.6 million bottles* in 2001) is the Americas (43.1 million bottles), which ranks far ahead of Asia (21.4 million bottles). It is almost totally unknown in Africa and Australasia. And since shoemakers' children aren't necessarily the best shod (as it makes more economic sense to sell the best), France only ranks third among cognac markets, with a mere 7.7 million bottles, far behind the United Kingdom (11.2 million) and, of course, the United States (40.4 million).
Often people think of cognac only as an after-dinner drink, which is the most traditional way of enjoying it. However, this brandy served with water, called

Cognac is suitable for all occasions, and won't turn your head if taken in moderation.

fine à l'eau*, was a popular French national aperitif until the 1950s. This tradition seems to be on the rise again, with cognac increasingly being served with sparkling water or soda water, a way of drinking it that is appreciated in the United States and Japan. Major hotel bars also serve cognac with ginger ale, cognac floaters (cognac poured in after the soda water, without being mixed), and cognac fizzes (with lemon juice). Barmen have appreciated the virtues of this alcohol for a long time, using it to make various cocktails. Here are just a few examples, recommended by the very serious BNIC*: Lancer-franc (cognac, orange juice, strawberry liqueur), Convergence (cognac, pineau, orange juice, strawberry liqueur), Sour (cognac, lime, cherry), Twelve-thirty (raspberry liqueur, cognac, chilled champagne, fresh raspberries), Hold-up (cognac, cane syrup, Malibu, orange juice, lemon juice), Sidecar (cognac, Cointreau, lemon juice), Amour Sanglant (cognac, cherry, vanilla liqueur, blood orange juice), and Romeo and Juliet (cognac, Pisang Ambon, Get 31, tonic). Finally, cooking is also one of the most agreeable, albeit indirect, ways to enjoy this spirit, which can be eaten as well as it can be drunk.

And, if the occasion arises, nothing need stop you from leaning against the bar of a café and ordering a "little" cognac (in volume, and, obviously, in quality) to accompany a strong Charentais coffee. Then, why don't you pour the cognac into the still-hot and just-emptied coffee cup, and enjoy the smooth mix of coffee and cognac aromas*. Some days, you've just got to keep bad company....

Cognac is an essential ingredient of many cocktails: try a "Lancer-franc" or a "Sidecar."

COOPERAGE

Pliny affirms that it was the Gauls who revealed the virtues of the barrel to Roman—and afterward to Barbarian—invaders, who until then had preferred to store their wine and oil in amphorae. Above all they appreciated the convenience of transporting barrels. They had not discovered the magic role wood plays in the maturation and aging* of wines and brandies, thanks to subtle interactions between the spirit and the tannins, and the major role played by evaporation and oxidation that only is possible with wood. The oak* cask is therefore indissolubly linked to vinification* and the production of brandies, even if shiny stainless-steel vats tend to crowd the cellars of the most prestigious of the French winemaking regions. For cognac, oak still ranks master, even if today it is sometimes difficult to find skilled artisans who can transform into barrels the rough staves, or shook, that come from the Limousin and Tronçais forests, planted under Louis XIV's finance minister Jean-Baptiste Colbert. To resolve this problem, certain major cognac firms produce their own barrels in their own cooperages, and have even purchased entire forests to ensure access to the best wood.

There is something admirable and enchanting about a cooper's know-how, his marrying of fire and wood, which wakes up ancient, deeply held memories. A cooperage is a vast building surrounded by piles of shook, delivered by the shook dealer, the first of the cooperage professions. Laid crosswise in a square shape, the wood is allowed to dry, or season, for several years in order to lose its bitterness and the greenness of its tannins. At the entrance to the cooperage, you feel as if you are on a blacksmith's doorstep: there are pounding mallets, dancing flames half hidden in the belly of a cask in the making—it's Vulcan in the country of Bacchus! Here, everything is made by hand, all machines being banished (except, perhaps, for making the hoops). The wood is split, never sawed, along the grain, with a clean, precise movement, so as not to alter the ideal porosity of the grain. Today a cooper still uses basic tools—an adze, a drawknife, a compass—that once were among the panoply used by carpenters and woodworkers.

The staves are assembled in a strange universe of shadows and light, steam

An adze, a tool used by the cooper for beveling the edges of the staves.

and smoke, from which a fragrance of burned wood escapes—although it is a very different odor from that of a wood fire. It is not the din that strikes the ears, but the rhythm of the mallets at work on the staves, a sound that deprives you of one part of your guide's explanations—a way perhaps of keeping secrets from the uninitiated. If you listen carefully, you will nevertheless learn that to begin making the barrel, the numbered staves are placed in a circle in a truss ring to form a "rose" (the image transforms the staves into petals), and that a fire of oak chips at the base of the barrel keeps them from breaking while being bent. The staves are kept damp and, using the heat of the flame, the cooper bends them into shape, drawing them together with metal or chestnut hoops. No glue, not a single nail is used—the pressure of the hoops on the staves is the only thing holding the precise assembly together, guaranteeing perfect watertightness.

The intensity of the toasting determines the spicy or smoky flavors that are not missed by the cellar master* when he tastes the brandy stored in the cask; he may even complain about excessive toasting, which is very fashionable in North America.

Charentais cooperage is universally recognized for its quality; it is considered the best in the world.

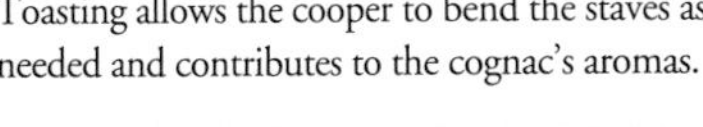
Toasting allows the cooper to bend the staves as needed and contributes to the cognac's aromas.

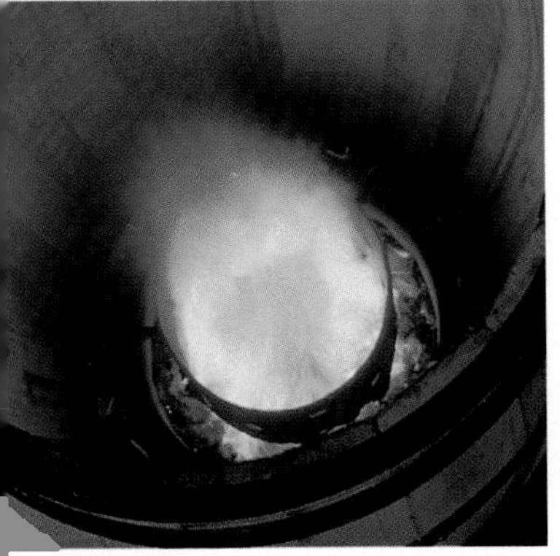

Copper

When you first enter the half-shadows of a cellar or distillery, often the coppery reflections of some utensil—a pitcher, a funnel—draw your attention, then, when the eye adjusts to the dim light, you see the red metal of the pot-still* head.

The shadows have disappeared from today's reputed distilleries, yet you still meet the bright shiny red of the pot-stills. The pot-still is made of a very pure copper, which is obtained by electrolysis and treated to tighten its pores, increase its mechanical resistance, and make it smoother and easier to clean.

This metal presents several advantages. Its malleability facilitates the making of complicated and precise forms. When heated by gas, its good conduction favors a regular distribution of the heat, so that the lees do not attach to the sides and get cooked. Copper resists corrosion well, although it can tarnish without proper maintenance. It reacts with fatty acids and sulfur compounds that can diminish the quality of the brandy. Copper also catalyzes complex reactions among different components of the wine. When heated, acids break down and oxygenize and then, being neither too volatile nor too

Copper is omnipresent in the making of a pot-still.

Spirit and copper: a marriage of two golds.

heavy, they pass with other derivatives into the heart of the *bonne chauffe**, or final distillation*, and contribute to the quality of the cognac.

Crus

Literally meaning "growth," used figuratively *cru* refers to a vineyard or a region, and here indicates the six regions of the cognac appellation. The *appellation d'origine contrôlée* (AOC) place-of-origin label system is a legal term based on the delimitation of a geographic production area, with the appellation decree stipulating production conditions concerning yield, authorized varieties, plantation density, conveyance methods, sugar content at harvest, alcohol content, and wine production. Respecting these regulations* ensures the continued character* and the quality of the appellation, in this case of cognac.

The delimitation of the cognac *crus* is the result of a gustatory tradition that dates back to the eighteenth century, and was itself the origin of the delimitation of the vineyards. Six *crus* have shared the delimited cognac region since May 1, 1909, when lawmakers made official what tradition had already established. The subdivision was based on observations made in the different production areas, which form roughly concentric circles, relating soil structure to corresponding characteristics in the final product. The various people involved in the winemaking process defined the names among themselves. They are listed here by decreasing value in the hierarchy of *crus* and starting from the center: Grande Champagne* (south of Cognac* and of Jarnac*), Petite Champagne* (farther south), Borderies* (to the north), Fins Bois* (encircling and farther north), Bon Bois (encircling), and finally Bois Ordinaires (to the northwest, toward Rochefort and La Rochelle). It is not common practice to mention these *crus* on the bottle labels, except sometimes for Grande Champagne, the vintage producing the finest, most delicate cognac with the most complex bouquet, and Petite Champagne, because of its similar-sounding name, which uninformed consumers could confuse with the other more prestigious vineyard. In practice, few cognacs are made from a single *cru*, and the cellar master* bases his choices on the particular quality of the wines from each domain in order to create a blend that is in keeping with the firm's particular style.

The classification of *crus* does not take into consideration the concept of grape variety*, or only in a general way. It is based first on the nature of the soil, the climate*, and the characteristics of the wines coming from a specific area.

Cuisine

The reputation of the cognac region stems from several products of the land, which inevitably inspire the regional cuisine. Local chefs and fine restaurants apply the best of their imagination to them, while mothers hand down regional culinary traditions from generation to generation. The two pillars of Charentais gastronomy are butter (Charente* butter gets an *appellation d'origine contrôlée* label) and snails (which here are called *cagouilles*). We could add a third, cognac (as whisky is in Scotland). It is certainly the spirit the most used by chefs and cooks throughout the world, finishing up in all kinds of sauces. Cognac inspires master chefs, who use it to deglaze the pan to make a fricassee, or to simmer a sauce over a low heat and so concentrate its wealth of aromas*, or to flambé fish, game, or a tart still warm from the oven. Of course, there is no sense using (some would say wasting) a top-of-the-line

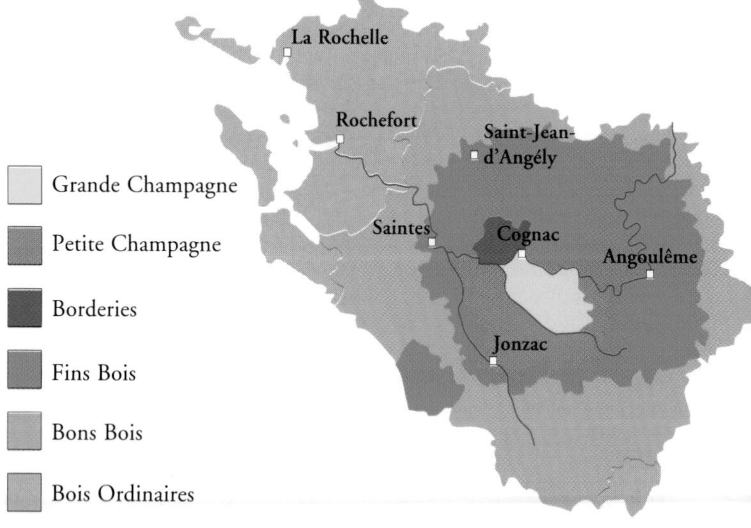

Map of the six crus making up the cognac appellation.

Many recipes include cognac in their ingredients.

*fine** cognac for cooking; but good ingredients give good results, and the most modest of cognacs will always be able to bring out the best flavors of the most delicate dishes. Certain firms have selected special cognacs, high in alcohol content, for top chefs to use.

Culture

"There is a place where France
is bacchante,
Where a liqueur of fire ripens
in full sunlight
Where sleeping volcanoes
shudder ardent ashes
Where the spirit of pure wine
equals that of the lava."
(Alfred de Vigny, 1852)

Celebrated by this poet's words, cognac is no ordinary beverage. It does not have the popular origins of other spirits, such as the calvados of the Normandy countryside or schnapps in Alsace, ancestral products that warm the belly and help one to confront life's adversities, not the least of which may be exhaustion from work. But you do not drink cognac to forget (except perhaps if you are a novelist on the downslide).

The discovery of cognac is presented either as a near-divine revelation, or the fruit of chance (depending on your metaphysics), which also, ever

L'ILLUSTRATION

Depuis 1765

le COGNAC HENNESS

porte à travers le monde le renom

du COGNAC

II. *1806 - " Encore une goutte de cognac, messieurs, et la victoire est à nous."*

so conveniently, coincided with an economic necessity: firstly facilitating export by concentrating the wine, then later exporting a high-quality product made by exceptional men to satisfy esthetic-minded consumers. From its beginnings, cognac has been a cultured product, an alcohol for connoisseurs and intellectuals, a nectar served at the end of the meal (in moderation of course) in the muffled atmosphere of a sitting room hazy with fine cigar smoke.

Very quickly, the name cognac acquired an international reputation, associated with a very French set of cultural criteria; with urbane conviviality founded upon a festive refinement as aristocratic as it was popular. The product's luxury seal comes more from the quality of its production than from its price, which in the long run is quite affordable for those who know how to be reasonable about the drink's age.

The tasting of cognac—like that of a fine wine—calls on the senses and leads to the use of an evocative vocabulary, which together indicate that we are in the realm of appreciation of a work of art. Many poets and writers were inspired to celebrate it with their particular talents. Pushkin and Dostoyevsky wrote about it, Charles Dickens had his hero Pickwick taste it. While novelist Alexandre Dumas was ordering it, poet Alfred de Vigny grew it and sold it in his Maine-Giraud manor. The French statesman Talleyrand taught his visitors the art of tasting it, while gourmet Antoine Brillat-Savarin found for it a place "at the table of men of taste." Poet François Porché said he "had been raised in the horror of alcoholism and the veneration of cognac," which he set out to celebrate as "a blessed, sacred, nearly divine liquor..., a spirit that smolders in the vine, bloats the grape, shines in the wine...and develops all of these spells."

In more recent times, Jean d'Ormesson, a journalist and member of the French Academy, wrote, "To speak of cognac is to evoke a world of refinement, of propriety in the art of receiving guests.... Cognac is a procession of conviviality." Native to Cognac, Jean Monnet, economist and father of Europe, remarks in his memoirs that, "The pride of belonging to the merchants of cognac...came more from the quality of the product itself than from its worldwide demand. This demand sanctions the quality." Also an expert in the matter, Robert Delamain concludes his *Histoire du Cognac* with these words: "In reality, cognac results from a happy set of circumstances, all exceptional, that make it a kind of natural prodigal son, an accident, a miracle." Maurice Hennessy, another expert and esthete, confirms this. "Cognac is the fruit of the love an individual brings to his work. The fruit of the whims of nature, of the circumstances of history, and the avidity of governments."

■ Cuts

In the process of distillation*, the cut, or *coupe*, refers to the operation that consists of isolating the first, second, and last runs in order to separate the best of the second *chauffe**, the "heart," that alone will be kept to make the cognac.

Cuts are the basis of blends.

In the blending* process however, the term refers to the mixing (a verb that may make things clearer for the neophyte, but would make a professional shudder) of the batches* of raw brandy classed by rounds based on their gustatory qualities, according to a numbered framework—the blending pattern. These cuts can be enormously complicated, and are always kept secret

The first step is called the first cut, or pre-cut. This mixture first spends some time in a barrel to acclimatize it and to ensure that it is evolving along the desired criteria. Then it is time for the second step. Based on the pattern indications, the first cuts are mixed among themselves; other brandies can be added. This is called the mother-cut.

After the new mixture is tasted and approved, and perhaps left in the barrel for a time, the next stage involves more blending or "marriages" among the different cuts, based on what the cellar masters* want to pass onto the last stage, called the final cut, which will be definitive. Yann Fillioux works as cellar master for Hennessy. His family has provided seven generations of cellar masters for the firm. He defines the process better than anyone, "Right from the start, our objective is to do exactly the same thing we have already done. We remix the cognacs among themselves, and from the moment we have the pattern, we are going to stick to it. On the first level, the pre-cuts are one part of the final blend. It all relies on being perfectly 'aligned' at this stage; if you are aligned during the first stage, you will be aligned in the following stage. Each stage is written out on a piece of paper, and we carry it out to scale, we taste, we compare it to what has been done previously in the same type.

"If it fits in with the style, we carry out the foreseen blend; if it is not, we blend again until it does. This way, we ensure continuity, with each stage being as close as possible to what we are aiming for."

Degree

In the distillation process, the term "degree" has a double meaning. First of all, it refers to the temperature level, which unleashes, among other things, the successive volatilization of various components of the wine. This is always indicated with a capital F for Fahrenheit and a capital C for centigrade. The term is also used in reference to the amount of pure alcohol, stated as degrees of proof spirit, calculated as a percentage of the volume based on a constant of one hundred. Proof in the United States is 50 percent alcohol by volume at 60°F (16°C), while in England proof is 52.10 percent by volume. On most cognac labels, alcohol content is generally expressed in "% vol," referring to the percentage of alcohol by volume, or ABV.

The strength of a cognac is measured with an alcoholometer.

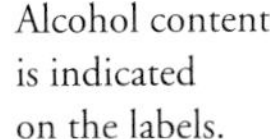

Alcohol content is indicated on the labels.

■ DISTILLATION

During fermentation, yeast performs a miracle, transforming the sugar in the grape-must into alcohol. What remains then is to collect this alcohol—this is the role of the distillation* process.

In addition to ethyl alcohol (ethanol), fermented grape-must contains glycerol (or glycerin), tartaric and malic acid, glucose and fructose, various other components and, of course, the 85 percent water* found in grapes. Because alcohol boils at a temperature lower (173°F/78.3°C) than water (212°F/100°C), when the must is heated, the alcohol evaporates first. All that is necessary is to recover it through condensation, now freed of the other components found in the wine. In Charente*, this operation is carried out in an imposing apparatus, made of gleaming crimson copper that matches the red ocher of the bricks surrounding it. This pot-still*, also known as the Charentais alembic, is the only still that allows for a double distillation (doubling*), one of the secrets of cognac. The same equipment serves to manufacture other spirits, notably AOC-classed Normandy calvados. Its enormous vat, with a capacity of 793 gallons (3000 litres), is heated over a high gas flame in a brick furnace. Wood was used in previous times, but it heated less well and required more handling, and coal also had similar drawbacks.

Preheated or not, the non-filtered must is introduced into the boiler and brought to alcohol's boiling point. The alcohol then evaporates into the still head that crowns the vat and whose form, specifically designed for this process, retains some esters (chemical compounds) and sends back others so they will come through in the heart of the *chauffe**. As the temperature increases, the alcohol escapes into the elegant swan's-neck pipe, which also has a carefully designed shape, moving on into the refrigerated coil, where it condenses in large droplets that are then collected.

Rid of its headings, the first ten litres, and of its tailings, the last one hundred litres, this first distillation produces between 198 and 210 gallons (750–800 litres) of a slightly cloudy

Steam rising from the boilers...

liquid that takes the name *brouillis**, and is 27 to 30 percent alcohol by volume. As nothing is wasted here, headings and tailings will generally be added to the next wine to be distilled. Once cooled off, this *brouillis* again goes into the boiler, along with other previously distilled *brouillis*, and will follow the same path a second time. This second distillation, limited to 660 gallons (2500 litres), takes the name of *bonne chauffe,* and is an operation that lasts about twelve hours. The distiller has to carry out a delicate operation—the cut* (not to be confused with the cuts made when blending*). This operation consists of separating out the first, most volatile headings (1 to 2 percent of the volume), too rich in alcohol and esters, before collecting the "heart"—a clear and limpid brandy, which is between 68 to 72 percent by volume and constitutes the future cognac. Then, when the alcoholometer drops below 60 percent by volume, he must set aside these "seconds," and the tailings, under 5 percent by volume. Headings and tailings will be used for

MARESTE
CONSTRUCTEUR
COGNAC

Collecting the "heart" as it comes out of the pot-still.

Facing page: Verifying the percentage of alcohol by volume, crucial to the quality of the cognac, occurs as it leaves the still.

the next *chauffe*, the former to be added to the grape-must, and the latter either to the grape-must or to the *brouillis*.
Some distillers pass the "seconds" again, thoroughly mixed, into the *brouillis*, while others prefer to incorporate them into a first distillation. This choice remains at the discretion of the distiller and is sometimes what distinguishes a brand, to such an extent that a cellar master* can often identify his brandies by carrying out a simple tasting.
The complete distillation cycle spans twenty-four hours, which explains why there is a bed in the distillery. To make a good product, the process must be slow and regular, just like the steady fall of the drops of spirit that are collected as they leave the coil's spout. There is no way to interrupt the process and come back the following morning!
So, consistency in the temperature is considered one of the criteria for making a quality cognac.
The producer (who is sometimes also the distiller) then uses the batches* of distillates thus made and separated, blending them as he judges necessary for the making of "his" cognac, based on the firm's specific criteria. All distillation must be completed by March 31 of the year following the harvest.
Many of the amounts mentioned here (those not stipulated by law), do not have a patented exactitude: every artist has his way of doing things and his own preferred quantities that are part of the production magic.

Alignment of stills in the distillery of a major cognac producer.

Doubling, or double distillation, is one of the secrets of cognac. The Charente pot-still was designed for this operation.

Doubling

One specific characteristic of cognac—and a certain number of other spirits made with the pot-still*—is that it goes through double distillation*; that is, it goes through the same apparatus twice. The first distillation of the wine produces the *brouillis**, a weak alcohol that only registers 27 to 30 percent by volume, far too low to make a powerful spirit. The second heating, called the *bonne chauffe**, more than doubles the alcohol content. The first distillates, the headings, and the last, the tailings, are eliminated. What's left is the "heart," which will form the basis of what will become a great cognac if, as with people, one knows how to bring out the best in it.

Storehouses on the banks of the Charente River.

Environment

When you stroll along by the wharves of the Charente* River in Cognac, the neglected aspect of the warehouses with their blackened and damaged walls may seem surprising compared to the treasures found inside. A local would tell you that this is normal. He would not talk about pollution (no bad words, please), but would tell you about the inevitable angels' share*, the evaporation that escapes the casks and, on the way, leaves a few traces on the walls (it is best not to think about what color these angels' wings might be). Although seemingly completely illogical, the argument is reasonable. A minuscule fungus feeds on the cognac vapors and proliferates wherever cognac evaporates. It's hardly surprising that, with such a diet, it is black. This fungus, *Torula compniacencis*, is barely perceived as a nuisance here. Other distillation* byproducts would present more serious threats to the environment

The angels' share leaves traces on the shutters and façades.

Today's cognac industry does not pollute the environment, as testified by the large fish population of the Charente River.

had effective solutions not been found to combat them.
A distilled grape loses only 10 percent of its matter. The remaining 90 percent makes up a residue called stillage. This is a serious potential pollutant due to its high content of oxidizable organic matter, which is avid for oxygen, and so capable of creating serious imbalances in watery environments by diminishing the oxygen content. Today, strictly monitored treatments (both aerobic and anaerobic) are used to process 99 percent of the stillage. Even the waste products are used. The profession* has set up a methanization unit that produces steam and electric power, and the residues from the process make an excellent fertilizer.

Esprit de Cognac

Only one product has the right to use the *appellation contrôlée* designation "*esprit de cognac*," and that is the distillate destined exclusively for the preparation of sparkling wines. It is obtained by a third distillation* of an *appellation contrôlée* cognac brandy. According to Article 1 of the decree dated March 11, 1938, this operation can only be carried out in an officially recognized Charentais pot-still*. Article 2, which stipulates the alcohol content, was modified by another decree dated October 3, 1957, authorizing between 80 and 85 percent by volume. It is considered fraud to reduce *esprit de cognac,* distilled to 85 percent by volume, by adding cognac.

Fine

Although today the waiters in the cafés on Paris's main boulevards may spend their days taking orders for a strong spirit of Scottish origin, their close ancestors in the 1950s found themselves regularly taking orders for *fine* (pronounced feen) with water, *à l'eau*. This was a happy time, when the best of French spirits, poured over ice and thinned with a little tonic, constituted the most prestigious of cocktails. But what is *fine*?

According to a law dated February 20, 1928, this term, which is synonymous with quality, is exclusively reserved for brandies made from an *appellation d'origine* (AOC) designated wine (which is the case with cognac) or cider, such as calvados. The law specifies that generic spirits cannot use this term. The text, judged to be too general by fraud-squad agents, was clarified by a ministerial circular dated March 30, 1928, which stipulates that the term "*fine*" should always be followed by "a geographic wine or cider appellation that is sufficiently known." In practice, the term *fine* designates a brandy of the *appellation d'origine contrôlée* cognac. All cognac would therefore be, in and of itself, *fine*. But no, this is not the case, because in order to use the label *fine*, followed by its specific geographic denomination, a cognac must represent a brandy made from one and the same *cru**. Thus, a Grande Fine Champagne indicates an AOC cognac Grande Champagne*, that is, blended with brandy issued exclusively from the Grande Champagne growth, a prestigious region producing cognac's *premiers crus*. In the same way, a Fine Fins Bois* is an AOC cognac blended with 100 percent Fins Bois.

The AOC designation Fine Champagne refers to a cognac blended only from brandy coming from the Petite* and Grande Champagne growths, with a 50 percent minimum of the latter (decree dated January 13, 1938).

Hennessy V.S.O.P. Fine Champagne is a big success abroad (this bottle is headed for Japan).

Folle Blanche

A close relative of the Folle Noire that you find in the Dordogne region in France, it has long been considered that the grape variety* Folle Blanche produces the most expressive cognacs, and therefore the most original ones. It was the predominant variety in the region before being decimated by phylloxera* in the nineteenth century. Even though it grafts without difficulty onto American vine stock, producers have since preferred Ugni Blanc*, which is less prolific and therefore less sensitive to rot.

Folle Blanche used to be the dominant grape variety for cognac production.

Glass

Bottling of cognac began in the nineteenth century, but at first was only done for a few prestigious customers. Until the 1860s, Charentes* brandy traveled mainly in casks. Bottling it was a minor revolution. Some producers, whose souls were steeped in local traditions, refused to do so, arguing that unlike wine, the spirit stopped aging* when its container was made of glass and sealed hermetically. How it goes in is how it comes out, which was and still is true. But the aim of bottling is more complex than that. First of all, the advantage is that the dealer knows the quality of the spirit he bottles, so he can guarantee it, an argument to which customers are always sensitive. The possibility of being able to see the product constitutes another strong argument in its favor. The cognac is no longer in a worn cask, which is supposed to contain the "nectar of the gods," but in glass containers, their transparency revealing the golden amber color* of the king of spirits, and each label ensuring publicity for the brand. The buyers would most certainly proudly show their friends as they honored them with a tasting from the divine bottle. The commercial and promotional impact was significant.

So the pine and cardboard of packing cases replaced the oak* of casks on the commercial routes, bringing with them manufacturers, cardboard factories, printing presses, and, of course, glassmakers.

In the storehouses, the oak continues to hide the slowly maturing cognac until the

Shipping cognac in cases of glass bottles (here with the encouragement of the singer Lili Pons in 1935) contributed to the success of cognac as an export.

Since 1894, it has been possible to make bottles mechanically, with a machine invented by Claude Boucher, a glass-maker in Cognac.

cellar master* decides it is time for it to be revealed in a bottle. Here, too, can be found an area reserved for the oldest of the brandies—the "paradise." This is an inner sanctum where the barrels, but also the demijohns, have witnessed a century, maybe more, go by. The glass demijohns contain just over 26 quarts (25 litres) of brandy, and protect cognacs over a half century old that, if left in a barrel, would lose the rest of their bouquet and their alcohol, to the point that they could not even be used to round off or help age younger brandies. Glass is a protection for these "endangered" works of art. Charentais call these demijohns "*dames-jeannes.*"

Grande Champagne vineyard.

Grande Champagne

The first recorded mention of Grande Champagne dates to 1713, in a pamphlet protesting high taxes. The Grande Champagne must therefore have been a recognized entity at this time, although neither it nor the other *crus** were mentioned in history and geography books nor in the administrative or parish registries. Its distinctive denomination thus relies solely on the production of a brandy of superior quality in the region of "*champs*," or fields ("*campania*" in a document dated 1259), as opposed to the surrounding woods. The qualifier "Grande" corresponds to the quality of the production, and not to the farmed surface.

The Grande Champagne area, located in the very heart of the production zone—its capital is Segnzac—covers 32,096 acres (12,989 ha.) of chalk-rich, well-drained, soil that produces, after slow distillation*, a very fine, rich, and elegant cognac.

Grape Varieties

Like all vineyards, those in Cognac are planted with a certain number of varieties, first chosen by winemakers, then through scholarly selections made by recognized scientists. All these varieties are harvested, for the most part mechanically, in October. It is worth noting that cognac's appellations, although primarily ruled by geographic considerations, are also linked to the grape varieties—all grapes used must be white wine grapes, with a 90 percent minimum of Ugni Blanc*, Colombard*, and Folle Blanche*.

There are also other secondary varieties grown in the Charente*, which can make up a maximum of 10 percent of the total—the Blanc Ramé (Meslier Saint-François), Jurançon, Montils, Sémillon, and Select.

The Ugni Blanc grape variety.

Inventory

Cognac is a living product that changes over time, depending on the wood of the casks. Every year, a substantial amount of the contents of each barrel evaporates—the angels' share*. So, to limit the angels' appetites, each year the casks must be topped up, a procedure that allows the actual quantities found in the *chais** to be measured. The major cognac firms have an inventory brigade responsible for this task. It involves not only noting quantities, which is what interests the tax authorities—that is, a physical count or stocktaking—but also tasting in order to monitor the quality and evolution of, perhaps, more than a thousand casks of brandy. At Hennessy, "the taking of the inventory lasts for five months, from May to September. It's the work of the cellar master* and his team, who control and guarantee the quality and consistency of the product. They taste each of the brandies in stock*, averaging 36 samples per session, two to five times a week." The time spent on these inventories is an essential investment. It allows the cellar master and his assistants to follow as closely as possible the evolution both of the batches* of brandy that have not been blended since they left the pot-still*, and those in the process of being blended. Knowing and comparing the flavors (odor plus aroma* plus savor) is vital to the development of future blends. This information enriches the gustatory archives of the producer, and confirms or negates previous observations made by the cellar master, who will note down the details for his own benefit, and for those who will follow him.

The inventory must be kept up to date.

Jarnac

The town of Jarnac enjoys a two-fold celebrity. It is known for the famous—and rather unorthodox—fencing maneuver implemented by its baron, Guy de Chabot, and for having been the birthplace of former French president François Mitterand. In 1547, during a duel against François de Vivonne in Saint-Germain-en-Laye, in the presence

Jarnac, the other major cognac town.

of King Henry II and his court, the intrepid baron of Jarnac hamstrung his adversary using a move that was more or less within the rules. This thrust ended up being particularly efficient, killing the adversary, and it went down into history as an expression, *coup de Jarnac*, which means something decisive but somewhat sly, a stab in the back. Perhaps it was from growing up with memories of this famous fencing move that François Mitterand acquired his formidable talents as a political duelist? Though it missed out on being more directly associated with the famous spirit, Jarnac is the second major cognac town, and here you will find some of the major distilleries and traders, whose *chais** line the right bank of the Charente* River.

Menu

To whet your appetite, let's put together a typical Charentais lunch menu. Start with a pineau* as an aperitif, unless it is warm out and you prefer a young cognac-on-the-rocks or with tonic, one of the numerous refreshing cocktails that have replaced the former *fine* à l'eau*. The meal will start with a dozen Marennes oysters served with a Charente* white wine, to be followed by steamed perch in a pineau sauce, or by snails in pastry with a cognac butter. The meal will continue with partridge breast in a Fine Champagne sauce, or a cutlet of veal from Chalais with pineau and morels. Or perhaps you would prefer the very typical chicken with pineau. We leave it to you to choose the red wine.
Don't forget to try the local cheeses, and then finish off the meal with a chocolate tart subtly laced with cognac, or an apple tart theatrically flambéed. After a good coffee, go for the perfect finish—a venerable old Fine Champagne, a bottle of the best cognac, ageless because it no longer has a label, but which "must date from my father's time…who left quite some time ago."

Napoleon

Napoleon left his mark wherever he went, even in places he never visited. Did he ever really stop in Charente* to merit his image on so many bottles* of cognac? It seems he did actually stop there, twice, in 1808 at Rochefort and at the island of Aix for an inspection, and then again there after Waterloo in 1815, just before giving himself up to the English. The story goes that, on this sad occasion, perhaps to raise his spirits, his supplier had a shipment of cognac sent to him, perhaps in the hope that he might depart for the New World (it is said that the fallen emperor had this in mind). The cargo fell into the hands of the English, who baptized their booty "Napoleon's cognac." The event opened London's doors to Napoleon's dealer, Emmanuel Courvoisier.

Throughout his reign, Napoleon kept coming into conflict with England and, in so doing, did not make life for the inhabitants of the Charente very easy. He thought the Continental System blockade would damage the British economy. Instead, the cognac market suffered greatly from it, as these neighbors-turned-enemies had for many years been special and loyal customers of the Charentais traders, whether buying salt, wine, or cognac. As for domestic consumption, the imperial court and some high dignitaries did order cognac, but

Rochefort. Napoleon stopped here before his departure for Aix in July 1815.

The Emperor, shortly before his final visit to Rochefort.

Napoleon's field-marshals barely had the time to taste this nectar, so busy were they running about Europe.

The return of peace under the Restoration launched trade again, and began a prosperous period for Cognac and the surrounding region. The Second Empire (that of his nephew, Prince-President Napoleon III, for a time fugitive in England, then prisoner at the Fort of Ham) was a veritable golden age for cognac. The splendor and pomp of the court and the whirl of crinolines were reflected in this "liqueur of the gods," as it was called by Victor Hugo when he tasted it during his exile in Guernsey.

But cognac owes most to diplomacy. The signing of the free-trade treaty with England transformed the fortunes of the Charentais traders. Unfortunately, the fall of the empire under Prussian boots, and most of all, the treacherous attack by phylloxera* in the latter part of the nineteenth century, again brought troubled times to the region.

In the meantime, as if honoring a member of the family,

A bottle of Napoleon cognac, an appellation that indicates a cognac with a minimum *compte* 6 age index.

our dealer Courvoisier adopted the famous image and the immortal name of Napoleon to adorn the labels of his bottles*. The entire industry followed suit, using the name to designate a cognac of a certain age (*compte* 6) and quality, worthy of the memory of a great man in a little hat.

Nobility and Clergy

The region of Cognac, which covers the three ancient provinces of Aunis, Saintonge, and Angoumois, is strewn with chateaux. In France, when you think of chateaux, you tend also to think of nobility. And in this part of France there is no shortage of blue blood. After it became definitively French in the thirteenth century, the Charentes* territory, familiar as it was with princely courts, attracted numerous coats of arms of illustrious nobility to its fiefs, where they would form their courts and found their lineages. Some still remain today.

The nobility played a key role in establishing the reputation of cognac, as here, at the chateau of La Rochefoucauld.

From the seventeenth century onward—cognac being a noble product—it was not considered demeaning to have the fruits of one's land "burned" in order to earn money. The process turned a good profit, in fact, despite the excessive zeal of the tax inspectors, who attempted to collect dues from the landed lords. The latter, arguing the privileges of their birthrights, refused outright to pay. Pleas and requests were sent to the king's court, defended by leading figures—the writer François de La Rochefoucauld, the cardinal and diplomat Melchior de Polignac, Rohan-Chabot—and supported by

Even though the monks were more interested in wine than in spirits, the abbeys (here the one at La Rochefoucauld) contributed to the success of cognac.

more than one hundred noble signatures.
Monks and priests had their pot-stills*, but were no more inclined to pay duty to the tax authorities, arguing that being in the service of God exempted them as much as rank by birth.

Nobility and clergy thus participated directly in the making of cognac's reputation by revealing its merits to the important individuals of the time, who wasted no time in giving in to its pleasures, ensuring a healthy future for this Charentais spirit.

Oak

Experience has shown that nothing is better than oak barrels for storing cognac brandies and aging* them. And as one can imagine, this oak must come from France—American oak has a bitter taste, while German, Austrian, and Russian oaks hold onto their tannins, so there is no interaction with the brandy.
Due to the quality of its grain, the only oak that is suitable for use in oak barrels is the French pedunculate oak from the forests of the Limousin and Tronçais regions, near the Charentes. These were planted by Louis XIV's finance minister Jean-Baptiste Colbert to supply timber for the royal fleet being built at Rochefort in the late seventeenth century. The wood's perfectly adapted

Open-air drying of shook.

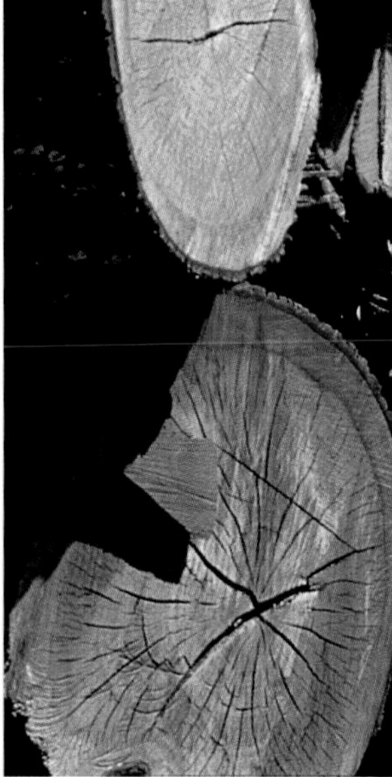
Blocks of felled oak, drying in the forest.

porosity optimizes interactions and oxygenation, which are primary contributors to the aging process.

The oak from the Limousin region, which has more extractable substances, gives a richer brandy, with more body; one that is capable of aging longer. The oak from the Tronçais in the Allier region is better for storing quick-aging cognacs. One-hundred-year-old trees imbue the spirit with the warm shades that attract the eye, aromas* that please the nose, and flavors that enchant the palate. It is for this reason that winegrowers, distillers, wholesalers, and merchants pay so much attention to having their master coopers produce the best casks, which generally hold 95 gallons or 360 litres, for their best cognacs.

Measuring an oak marked for cooperage.

The spirit will typically spend two years in a new barrel before being poured into one that had already held brandies, and so has been freed of the majority of its tannins. Although many of the common, everyday cognacs leave the barrel after thirty months, the best, from Champagne*, can stay in oak for as long as ten years, and some even longer, to an upper limit of fifty years, beyond which time, perfectly matured, they are stored in demijohns.

Each of the major brands has this kind of treasure, sealed as it should be in a specific, protected area of the *chai** that is

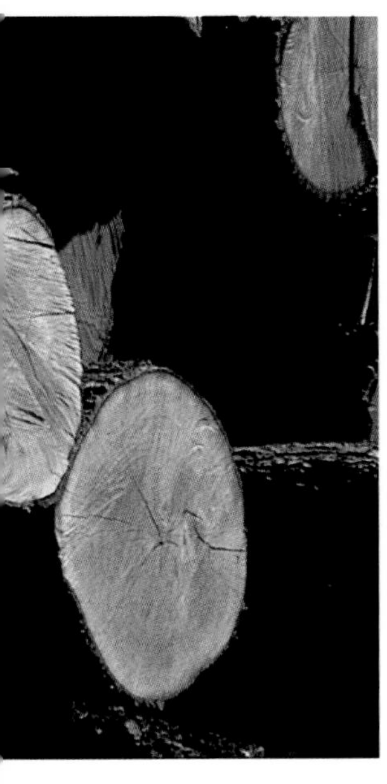

Petite Champagne

With 37,767 acres (15,284 ha.) of vineyards, this Champagne growth, which encircles Grande Champagne*, its big sister, to the southwest and southeast, and which covers a larger surface area, produces a cognac with stronger floral and fruity notes. Under the label Fine Champagne, it seems somehow to "tease" the perfection of the "Grande." Petite Champagne brandies are often used in blends for their personality. The slight differences found among its brandies could be explained by the fact that there is a little less chalk in the soil, and the area has a more varied aspect.

known as the "paradise." Stored on ground level, the barrels, three deep and four or five high, give the storehouses an impressive appearance. The barrels found at the far ends of these lines carry the initials C H, which are generally written on them in chalk. These are the *chanteaux*, which are barrels containing very old cognacs. These cognacs are sacrificed to maintain the levels of the other barrels, whose contents evaporate as they mature, making up the famed "angels' share*." This very old cognac plays an essential role in creating the marketable product, rounding off the blends while diminishing the rancio*, a characteristic flavor of old cognacs and a mark of prestige in exceptional products.
Here, there are no underground cellars—in fact, changes of weather and temperature contribute favorably to the aging process.

Winegrowers have grown healthy, vigorous new vines from American rootstock resistant to phylloxera.

Phylloxera vastatrix, the parasite that wreaked havoc on the entire French vineyard toward the end of the nineteenth century.

Phylloxera

No history of French vineyards would be complete without a mention of phylloxera. Introduced accidentally via American grapevines, this parasitic vine disease attacked Charentais vineyards from 1872, striking around the area of Chérac and Cognac.

A minuscule, burrowing plant louse, *Phylloxera vastitrix*, attacks the roots of the grapevine, and there is no treatment available to combat it. It quickly turned into the entire profession's* nightmare. Powerless to stop its proliferation, a drastic solution was decided upon—to uproot the all the vineyards. Of the region's 690,000 acres (280,000 ha.), which in 1870 made up the largest of the French vineyards, barely 124,000 acres (50,000 ha.) remained in 1894.

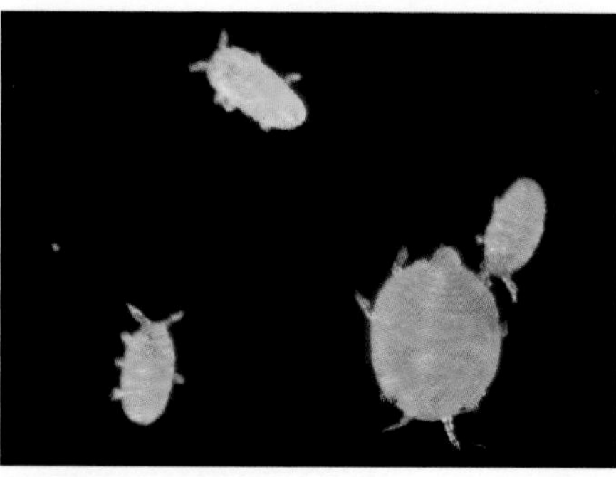

However, a defense was found—to graft *Vitis vinifera* varieties onto native American rootstock, which is naturally resistant to the parasite. In 1880, a first attempt failed: the rootstock was unable to adapt to the chalky soil. The Charentais had to send a special expedition to the United States in order to find adapted strains.

Although the vines do not live as long as they used to using this system, they do have better resistance to diseases without affecting the quality of the grapes. The same varieties as before are cultivated, and these can now be grafted onto this rootstock. It was at this time that the Ugni Blanc* variety largely replaced the formerly used varieties of Colombard* and, in particular, Folle Blanche*(the latter being sensitive to gray rot because of a too-high yield). As the Ugni Blanc variety grows later in the season, it is better protected from spring frosts.

During those troubled years, people did whatever they could to survive, and fraud of all kinds flourished, both in production and in appellations. The consequences were disastrous for the entire industry, which was hit by poor sales due to consumer mistrust. Most of today's strict regulations date to this period. By cleaning up the industry, customer confidence was regained, so safeguarding the future of cognac.

Pineau

The Charentais are certainly very lucky. Just as cognac is said to have been discovered by chance, pineau is also said to be the product of happenstance. The legend goes that in 1589 a Charentais winegrower absentmindedly poured grape-must into a barrel of *eau-de-vie* (which at this time was not yet called cognac). He left the barrel in his master's storehouse and forgot about it. A few years later his lord needed to store a big harvest. He came across the barrel in his storehouse, which now contained a marvelous beverage: limpid, golden in color, smooth to the taste, but with body. Born by chance, the recipe was then perfected, written down, and reproduced loyally by generations of winegrowers. White pineau is made from the same grape varieties* as the must that is later distilled into cognac, while Cabernet Sauvignon, Franc, Merlot, and Malbec varieties produce rosé pineau.

The *appellation d'origine contrôlée* (AOC) place-of-origin label system is based on the delimitation of a geographic production area, with the appellation decree stipulating production conditions. Pineau des Charentes must respect strict regulations concerning yield, authorized varieties, plantation density, conveyance methods, sugar content at harvest, alcohol content, and vinification*. Respect of these regulations ensures the continued personality and the quality of the appellation. A commission, formed by the INAO (National Institute of Appellations of Origin) and the professional organization of the appellation, inspects samples of the wine and accords or withdraws authorization. Only accredited products can be marketed under the name Pineau des Charentes, which the decree dated October 12, 1945 (modified in 1998) granted only to wines produced in the production area of the Charente department, the Charente-Maritime department, and two enclaves in the departments of Dordogne and the Deux-Sèvres. White and rosé pineau result from blending—*mutage*—in oak casks of three-fourths fresh grape-must and one-fourth one-year-old cognac, with no more than 16 to 22 percent alcohol by volume. The addition of the

White and rosé pineau.

The Charentais vineyard not only produces grapes for cognac, it also produces those used to make Pineau.

alcohol stops the fermentation of the must. The grape-must—which results from light pressing—and the cognac must come from the same estate. The maturity of the grapes must be perfect in order to retain the natural richness of the juice, which must contain at least six ounces of sugar per quart (170 g of sugar per litre), for 10 percent alcohol. The adding of sugar is strictly forbidden. The annual harvest produces around 2,641,720 gallons (100,000 hl), divided nearly equally between white and rosé, with slightly more of the former. This fills more than 12 million bottles*, of which nearly a fourth are exported, mostly to Belgium, a long-time lover of pineau and Charente wines.
Pineau that is labeled *vieux,* or old, must spend at least five years in the cask, and *extra-vieux*, ten years. Since 1949 the industry has been organized under the professional organization, Comité National du Pineau des Charentes (CNPC).

Pot-still

A pot-still, or alembic (from the Arabic word, *al-anbiq*), refers to an apparatus used to distill a fermented product such as wine, cider, barley, or hops, in order to extract the alcohol (another Arabic word). It is of Egyptian origin, and dates back to 3000 B.C. when it was used to obtain kohl, a preparation made from antimony and used by Egyptian women to darken their eyelids. Nearer to our times, the Egyptian-born Greek alchemist Zosimus (300 A.D.) published a treatise on the subject, illustrated with helpful diagrams. The apparatus already comprised the

three major parts that make up the Charente pot-still:
1. The boiler, in the shape of an onion or a gourd, holds the liquid to be distilled. It is placed on a furnace, which heats the liquid until the alcohol boils at 173°F (78.3°C).
2. The still head or hat is a collecting chamber above the boiler that traps the evaporating alcohol.
3. A coiled pipe dips into a receptacle holding cold water; the drop in temperature causes the alcohol vapor to condense into fine droplets, to be collected in liquid form at the exit.
The Arabic pot-still was first introduced into Europe when the Moors invaded Spain, and at the time of the Crusades. Scientific exchanges took place between Arabs in Cordoba and the professors at the University of Montpellier, inspired by the work of Arnáu de Vilanova.
The pot-still's early retorts (distillation* chambers) were made of earthenware, glass*, or bronze. Later they were fabricated out of pure copper, and over time the pipe leading off the still-head evolved into the elegant swan's-neck shape we find today. The furnace was later enclosed, to heat more effectively, and a preheater was sometimes added. This chamber was designed to preheat the wine prior to the first distillation, following the path taken by the alcohol vapor. This apparatus, described in all its simplicity, does not need to be changed before the doubling*, or second distillation, a very important procedure in the making of quality cognacs that merit their reputation and meet the requirements of its AOC (*appellation d'origine contrôlée*) label.

The "heart" of the *bonne chauffe*, or second distillation, as it leaves the still.

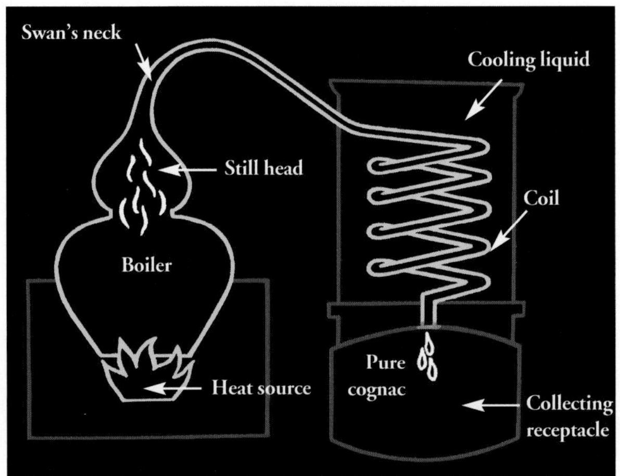

Explanatory diagram for a pot-still.

■ PROFESSIONS

In the pyramid of cognac-related occupations, the dealer appears at the top. This does not mean he is the most important—they all work together, as they are all part of the same chain—but he is the last person involved. He is the one who finds customers, attracts them, processes orders and, above all, sells the cognac. This role is often linked to that of distiller-producer, and some even combine it with the roles of owner-winemaker-grower for appellations that are not subject to a place-of-origin label (AOC). If the owner of a vineyard cultivates the grapes, he becomes the winegrower. As for the winemaker, he cultivates the vineyard and is de facto a winegrower, even if he does not own the vineyard.

The profession of distiller is specific. He owns the Charentais pot-still*, registered under a number with the tax authorities, and has received authorization to "burn" or distill the wine of the region delimited by the appellation cognac. If he grew and harvested the wine, he is a distiller-winegrower for that particular brandy, and simply a distiller for the wines that come to him from elsewhere, although of course they are always from the Cognac region.

A cellar master at work.

There are also the titles of *bouilleur* and *bouilleur de cru**, which refer to distillers with slightly different legal rights.

To be a producer in winemaking means to mature the brandies (or wines, in other regions), that is to say, to keep them while they age, providing them with the care that they need. The cellar master*, who is also the blending* master, is the finest example of a producer.

The winegrower's attentive care contributes to the quality of the finished product.

The dealer is the one who is in contact with the most important of all the factors in the process: the customer. The largest cognac houses, although they do monitor the majority of the operations involved in the production of their cognac are, above

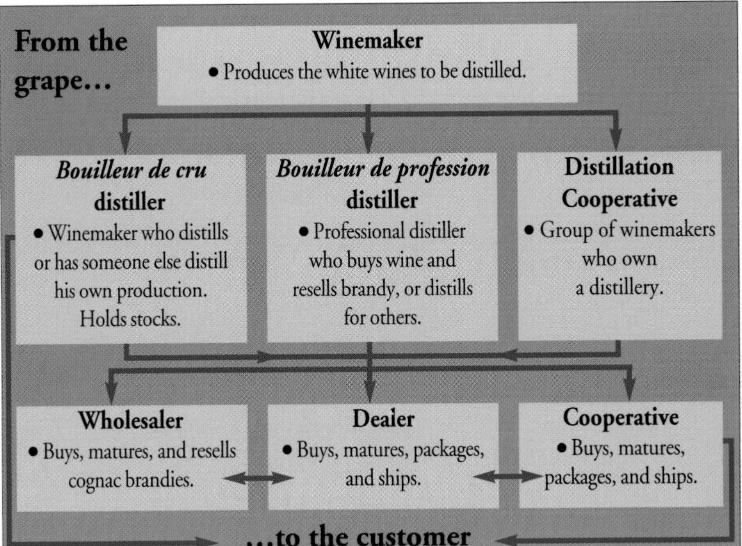

all, commercial companies. Their company managers are primarily dealers, and often have been for generations. The commercial networks they have woven over the years have ensured that their brandy is sold throughout the world, and have made cognac the most well-known spirit in the world.

Cognac-Related Professions

In addition to the 3000 or so people working for distillers and shipping companies, the following cognac-related occupations can be found in the area:

Year	2000/2001	1999/2000
Cooperage	783	516
Glassmaking	573	679
Cork-making	110	73
Cardboard and printing	910	1040
Brokers and boilermakers	516	435
Forwarding agents, transport, insurance	407	377
Safety, environmental protection	26	28
Professional organizations and Oenology laboratories	95	122

In the delimited cognac region, the number of jobs can be estimated at 3000.
There are around 8000 vineyard estates producing the Charente white wine that is allowed to be used for the appellation cognac.
If you add the husbands and wives of the winegrowers and permanent employees, the number reaches 15,000 people working in winegrowing and involved in the activity of producing cognac.
If you include the families of these working people, that makes around 55,000 inhabitants whose livelihood depends on the product, out of just under 900,000 people living in the region.
Source: BNIC, 2001.

Rancio, an aroma characteristic of old cognacs.

Rancio

One of the terms that is specific to cognac-making is "rancio." The word evokes the acrid flavor and the moldy taste that fatty substances, such as butter, develop over time. Yet, what is a serious fault with butter, making it inedible, becomes an asset in cognac; it is the sign of a venerable spirit. The odor becomes even nobler when an oenologist tells you it is an organoleptic element, which means it is an aromatic component that the nose and palate discern in cognacs over the age of fifteen. Rather than speak about a rancid flavor, he will tell you there is a touch of undergrowth in there, of mushrooms, with hints of walnut and raisins, making the odor more beautiful. The chemist will tell you more prosaically that rancio is due to a molecule, ketone, that results from the combination of the wine's fatty acids with the tannin and the lignin of the oak* casks. The capillarity of the wood allows oxygen to come into contact with the brandy's chemical components, and the basic acids decompose, notably lauric acid (which is particularly present in young brandies) into ethyl laurate. When isolated this has a characteristically rancid odor. During the aging* process, this substance mixes with other ketones from other oxidized fatty acids and finds itself greatly mellowed. Associated with typical fragrances developed by the cognacs of its age, it has a singular aroma*, which a seasoned taster will identify as raisins, sugared apricots, and a hint of concentrated vanilla, a drop of old port, and a smidgen of butter... Charente* butter, of course.

Reduction

The habit of drinking wine straight is not that old; Napoleon cut his Chambertin with water*, as did a number of his contemporaries. Cognac vocabulary has its nuances however. When a brandy is "cut*," it will never be cut with water, but with one or several other brandies. To add water to cognac, other than when you drink it, is to *reduce* it. In fact, it is to lower the alcohol content to 40 percent by volume, the compulsory minimum, that you see on the labels. This level can be reached naturally, right out of the cask, but only after fifty years at best. A reduction (completely legal and traditional) is thus imposed on products that have not reached this old age. The operation is carried out with great care. A first mix of cognac and distilled water is made to reach 27 percent

Pure alcohol or water? When the distillate leaves the pot-still*, one could wonder. It is only over the years, by way of subtle interactions between the oak* and the spirit, that the brandy takes on the characteristic amber color* of old cognacs. At the initial stage, only an experienced professional can foresee the qualities of the future fine cognac.

by volume. This is called the *faible* or *petite eau,* and it will be set aside to "rest" for some time before then being incorporated carefully into the cask that is to be reduced. Here, again, the operation might be carried out bit by bit until the desired strength is reached.

Another occasion on which brandy can be reduced with very pure water is when tasting a maturing cognac when it is still very young—from the time it leaves the still through to *compte* 3. Here, the demands of the tasting take priority. The alcohol, in the full strength of its youth, is too present in the nose and palate, masking any developing aromas*. Clear water and the developing spirit just out of the still look exactly the same, and when the reduction is carried out very delicately at this stage, a totally colorless liquid will allow professionals to determine the primary characteristics of the products that will be the future of the firm.

Reduction aims to lower the alcohol content.

Regulations

Cognac is not only the best spirit in the world, but without a doubt also the most regulated. Regulations apply to all stages of its production, beginning with its place of production. Cognac can only be made from wines produced in municipalities listed in one of the six recognized *crus** that form the appellation cognac (decree dated May 1, 1909, modified January 13, 1938).

The grape varieties*, all white, must correspond to those stipulated in the decree dated May 15, 1936, modified on May 11, 1971, in precise proportions: a majority (90 percent) must be Ugni Blanc*, Folle Blanche*, and Colombard*, while 10 percent can be Blanc Ramé (Meslier Saint-Francois), Jurançon, Montils, Sémillon, or Select (decree dated January 13, 1938, modified). On the other hand, pruning is not regulated. The dates of the harvest, which can be mechanical or manual, are set by order from the prefecture. The decree dated May 15, 1936, modified, forbade the continuous screw-type press and the addition of sugar, or "chaptalization."

The distillation* *must* be concluded by March 31. The capacity of the boiler, always made of copper, is set at 793 gallons (3000 litres) and must contain only 660 gallons (2500 litres) for the second distillation. Of course, each litre of alcohol, produced exclusively by doubling* in a Charentais pot-still*, is recorded, with its date, for the age index* (order dated February 20, 1946). The administration then leaves it to age in peace, in the exclusively oak* casks, except if somebody decides to remove the cognac from the *chai** and put it on the market before it turns thirty months of age. If this were to occur, the fraud-squad would act, according to the order dated February 20, 1947. Such a cognac would not be able to receive its *acquit jaune d'or**

The regulations allow for both manual (following page) and mechanized (above) harvests.

certification, effectively its identity card—which is now computer-generated, but still has a yellow, or *jaune*, border. More detailed than an individual's identity cards, this alone allows the cognac to travel (law dated August 4, 1929 and article 474 of the General Tax Code).

Finally, to be marketed, cognac must genuinely measure 40 percent alcohol by volume—except in very rare circumstances with very old cognacs—as listed on the label, where one must also find the regulation information indicating the age of the youngest brandy that was used in its blend (decision dated August 23, 1983 of the government commissioner with the BNIC*).

It is not compulsory to identify the *cru*, except for the use of *fine**, placed before the reference name (Fine Fins Bois*, Grande Fine Champagne*) to specify that the brandies of this cognac come uniquely from the *crus* mentioned.

The appellation Fine Champagne, without Grande or Petite, indicates a cognac blended from at least 50 percent Grande Champagne brandy, and the rest exclusively from Petite Champagne*.

Remedy

Brandy is also known as *eau-de-vie* or "water of life" in English, and indeed the spirit is supposed to encourage life. The ancients attributed almost

1930 Australian advertisement presenting cognac as a remedy.

supernatural virtues to it, impressed as they already were by the mysterious, nearly alchemical, processes involved in producing it.

Arnáu de Vilanova, in a scientific study dating to around 1250, justified the term *aqua vitae.* Around 1300, Raimundo Lulio, a Catalan theologian and philosopher, called it "divine liqueur," considering it a gift of God. Others, incredulous or suspicious of this liquid that was as clear as water, but that caught fire on contact with flame, spoke of "firewater." To them, this firewater seemed to be the product of witchcraft. In the fifteenth century, after some in-depth studies, it was recommended as a remedy for reducing pain, watering eyes, bad breath, suppurating wounds, frostbite, and bites from poisonous "*bestes,*" not to mention, of course, incurable diseases. *Eau-de-vie* became a remedy, a medication taken with pleasure once its flavor had been improved with aromatic plants. In 1573, Liebault recommended it for "*estomach*" aches.

On ships, it was a popular remedy for scurvy, although certainly less effective than onions and lemons. In more recent times, reputed to fight gangrene, cognac often served to disinfect wounds, or in the countryside for the very relative asepsis of surgical

TRADE MARK

We guarantee our brandies to be pure and genuine COGNAC BRANDIES of the finest quality, adapted for medical use. They have been stored and shipped under the ACQUIT RÉGIONAL COGNAC, which is a special guarantee, created by the French laws and only applicable to brandies made solely from wines produced in the COGNAC DISTRICT.

A Certificate signed by FRENCH EXCISE OFFICERS states these facts and accompanies the shipment including this bottle.

CERTIFIED COPY of the said Certificate can be obtained on application to our U. S. representative, Messrs SCHIEFFELIN & C°, New York, providing number and marks on case referred to are duly mentioned

Jas Hennessy & C°

A certificate testifying to the therapeutic qualities of cognac. This permitted its sale during Prohibition in the United States.

Merlot is one of the red grape varieties being reintroduced to produce Charente wines.

instruments, or to revive a patient who had fainted. In 1832, it was used to help fight the cholera epidemic that hit London and Paris. At the time, cognac was considered a good restorative. In 1910, in Asian countries, and notably in China, an increase in sales followed a publicity campaign that boasted of its virility-improving qualities. In the United States during Prohibition a clever dealer, to save his market, claimed his cognac to be "medicinal," and managed to continue exporting it. The English doctor Charles Russ recommended it to fight fever, flu, and pneumonia. Its virtues as a stimulant and cardiac regulator have been recognized, and someone went so far as to recommend it to athletes as "caloric and energetic nourishment necessary for muscular effort."

It is true that you cannot get a more natural product. Made from grapes, and produced without additives of any kind, cognac receives a maximum of attention and care, and is thoroughly certified and guaranteed. Such a product can only be good for the health, if taken in moderation.

Restructuring

The cognac industry is fortunate to have large surface areas, and high production, sales, and stock* figures (representing 87 million gallons or 3.3 million hectolitres in 2001). Recently the entire industry has been considering restructuring in order to employ these resources more efficiently and to greater profit. An ambitious conversion program of the Charentais vineyards proposes replanting more than 17,000 acres (7000 ha.) of today's Ugni Blanc* vineyards (out of just under 198,000 acres, or 80,000 ha.) with grape varieties* for regional table wines by 2006. The operation has been named VPC 2006, the three letters corresponding to

The Sauvignon grape variety has been reintroduced under the new Charente vineyard restructuring program.

vin (wine), pineau*, and cognac, a trio of the future. Remember that before the "discovery" of cognac, the area produced a lot of wine; entire fleets searched it out to distribute throughout Holland and Scandinavia, and even to the Baltic and Canada. For a time, these wines even graced the tables of the French and English courts. Knowing that between 136,000 and 148,000 acres (55,000–60,000 ha.) are basically sufficient for the production of cognac, the agricultural chambers of the two Charente* departments, along with other institutional partners, decided to support the cognac industry in a restructuring plan, with the financial support of the national government.

Out of the nearly 400 million gallons (15 million hl) of French table wine produced, the Charentes would only add about 2.6 million gallons (100,000 hl). These winemakers will have to prove that they still know how to produce quality wines. This is the targeted niche, and the two agricultural chambers of the Charentes

Young grapevines (right): part of the restructuring program.

The production of quality white wines is the goal of the VPC 2006 operation.

have implemented a promotional program handled by the Committee for Diversification, whose task it is to suggest to winemakers the different possibilities open to them—conversion to table wine production, diversification into pineau, or removing the vines temporarily or permanently—and to provide them with information concerning the aid they can receive.

Replanting has already begun with whites (Sauvignon and Chardonnay) and reds (Merlot, Cabernet-Sauvignon, Gamay, Cabernet-Franc). The future will tell whether the operations are completed successfully, but it is certain that the industry shares a common goal, and its know-how is the best guarantee of success.

Safety

Since the very beginning of brandy-making, fire has been a much-dreaded threat associated with its production. For a long time cities have limited the production of the spirit within their boundaries.

Bordeaux resolved the problem early on with a straightforward ban on "making or having made any firewater in the city." In 1514 the guild of sauce-makers, café-owners, vinegar-makers, and distillers was established in Paris, with distillers later splitting off into their own guild in 1537, so different and specific were the interests of their profession*. Apart from the danger of fire, which justified inspections in itself, a rudimentary inspection of the finished product was also undertaken. The presence of furnaces to heat the wine in immediate proximity to the stored alcohol required specific precautions: notably, that there should be a waterway nearby. This served a dual purpose: it supplied water*, which was necessary in any case, and it allowed for the evacuation of the residues of distillation* known as stillage.

Because of the aging method, producers always have a lot of spirit stored in barrels on their premises.

On Charentais farms, the distillery, although adjoining the buildings, is found at their extremity, whereas in Normandy, where wood beams were used in house-building, the distillery has always been separate.

Nowadays, with safety having become a priority, draconian rules have been laid down. In the large distilleries, specially trained safety teams provided with high-performance equipment are trained to intervene very quickly. Hennessy's firefighting equipment, for example, would be sufficient to protect a small town. As for prevention (installation standards, bans on smoking) and protection (fire-resistant materials, smoke detectors and smoke vents, area cut-offs), all possible measures are applied. The same

rules apply in the *chais**. Nobody wants to see his stocks go up in smoke. After all, enough is lost anyway to the angels' share*.

Stocks

In the cognac delimited region, in 2001, the quantity of brandy stored in casks in *chais** amounted to over 87 million gallons (3.3 million hl) of pure alcohol, or the impressive number of 1.165 billion bottles*, which nevertheless represents no more than seven years' production, taking evaporation into consideration.

The total harvest of white cognac wines for 2000 reached 215,237,861 gallons (8,147,641 hl vol), of which only a third, in accordance with current regulations*, was distilled, making 8,578,087 gallons (324,716 hl) of pure alcohol.

Stock management has always required a precise accounting system.

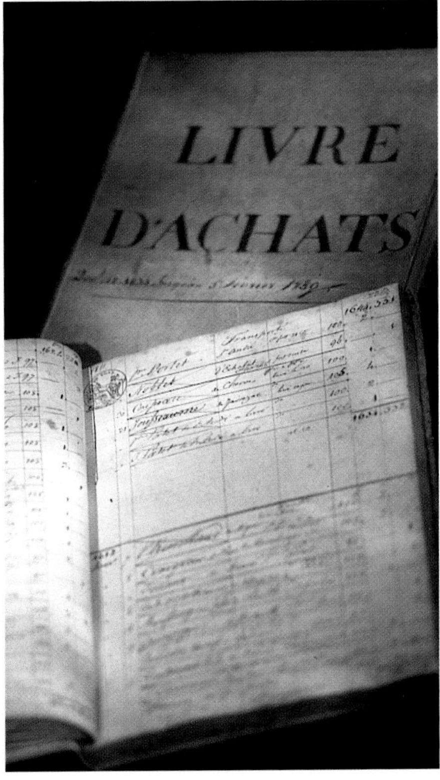

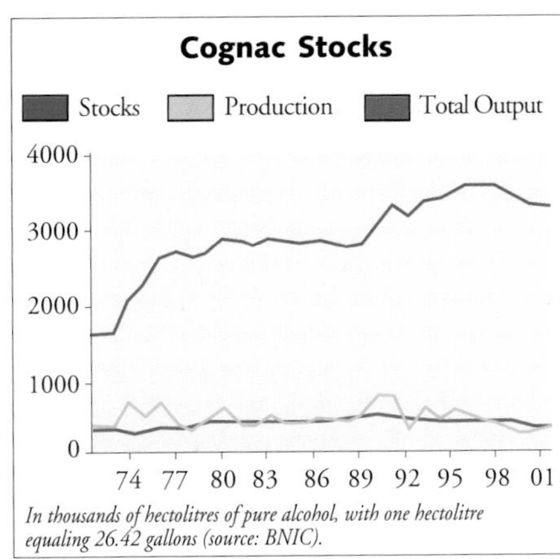

In thousands of hectolitres of pure alcohol, with one hectolitre equaling 26.42 gallons (source: BNIC).

Cigars and cognac are made to be enjoyed together.

Tasting

There are two kinds of tasting. One consists of all the visual, olfactory, and gustatory tests the cellar master* carries out on the different batches* of cognac produced; the other is the judgement and appreciation of the customer, who is often used to the taste of "his" cognac, and who boasts of its merits with pride, as if he had contributed to them personally.

The cellar master must be attentive to how the spirit evolves over the years. Based on his observations, he will take certain measures and make decisions about such major operations as blending* and bottling. As an experienced professional, he will pinpoint the qualities and weaknesses of cognacs in the making, encouraging the former, correcting the latter.

The customer's tasting is much more individual: it is an amateur's tasting, with all the subjectivity that supposes. There is no table with a range of labeled samples; there is no alignment of official tasting glasses*, elegant tulip-shaped receptacles that open up to allow the aromas* to develop. Nor are there those surprising glasses whose intense blue color hides the brandy's color* from the taster, so that his palate remains influenced only by the flavor and not by the quality of the color. What counts here, above all, is conviviality, settling down in comfortable chairs with friends after a meal, perhaps by the fireside and with a cigar. This tasting, *à la française*, friendly as it may be, does not allow for

Blue glasses prevent tasters being influenced by the color of the cognac.

comparisons, because more often than not there is only one bottle of cognac.
With the classic brandy glass, preferably crystal and warmed in the palm of your hand, you take the time to admire this nectar of the gods, to judge its smoothness by the tears and legs that form on the inside of the glass. You observe its transparency by lifting it to a light source, appreciating its amber color, whose shade is often judged, sometimes hastily, as a guarantee of age. Then you sniff it several times, with small inhalations, and discuss it with others, exchanging comments about the color and the aromas. Then the palate comes into play: you take a small mouthful, and keep it in your mouth before swallowing it with your eyes closed. At this moment, the aromas begin to reveal themselves; first perceived in the nose, you then analyze the savors, the fruity notes that rise in the mouth and burst, like fireworks. You run your tongue back over the palate to lose nothing of the precious nectar. You discover the fleeting touches of dried flowers, the different savors so difficult to define for the non-specialist, over which you debate, argue, feel indignant, or even joke. And then there are other impressions—the crisp freshness of green apples, a fragrance of rose, a musky note of undergrowth, a touch of apricot or peach, a dash of ripe fruit, a pinch of pepper, of spices, of herbs, of hazelnut, or

Tears and legs are signs of quality in a cognac.

Mechanical harvesting.

of almond. Blossoming fragrances fill your mouth and linger on and on, an ode to the imagination, a voyage to a land of dreams, undergrowth, and islands.

"And then, Sir, you set down your glass and speak about it," said the French statesman Talleyrand to a Russian diplomat, who drank his cognac as if it were a vulgar vodka, according to André Castelot. The tasting of cognac is an art, almost a ceremony, ignored in many areas of the world, even where cognac is drunk in greater quantities than in France. Tasting is also the expression of a very Epicurean tradition, and at the same time, it is the greatest tribute that you can pay to the efforts made by an entire profession*, which has labored hard to present a beverage meriting the envied title of best spirit in the world—itself a fine reflection on French culture.

Ugni Blanc

Also called the Saint-Émilion of the Charentes*, because of its origins in the Bordeaux region, today Ugni Blanc is

Ugni Blanc has become the dominant grape variety in the wine used to make cognac.

Pruning is one of the processes that contributes to quality vinification.

the major grape variety* of the cognac production region. In addition to resisting disease well, Ugni Blanc is also less sensitive to the spring frosts, as this variety grows rather late in the season.

The grape has two main qualities—high acidity, and a large proportion of yeast that accelerates the fermentation of the must. In Charente, it produces a wine with a low alcohol content (8 percent by volume on average) that contributes to the alcoholic balance of the double distillation* and to the development of an expressive cognac. The very sunny years, when the wine spontaneously comes out to be 12 percent by volume, are considered to yield poor cognacs.

After the phylloxera* crisis, Ugni Blanc progressively supplanted Folle Blanche*, a variety more resistant to grafting onto American vine stock.

Vinification

As cognac is made through the distillation* of a wine made from white grape varieties*, of which 90 percent are Ugni Blanc*, it is useful to know how this wine is made.
Vinification takes place right after the harvest, which for the most part today in the Charente* is mechanical. It is a classic white wine vinification process for very healthy grapes, and includes their stems and stalks. The process must be quick, without maturing, to avoid all oxidation, which means the distillation is not really of a wine, but rather of a grape-must, or a very young wine. The use of pneumatic or low-pressure horizontal presses ensures that the skin bursts correctly and, above all, does not crush the seeds. That is why regulations forbid the continuous screw-type press.
The addition of sulfur—"sulfating"—and sugar—"chaptalization"—are not tolerated, so the product remains natural. Natural decantation clarifies it, making use of the natural effect of gravity over a period of a few hours. Thus cleared of its solid wastes, the clarified juice is stored in stainless-steel vats, where it can ferment completely under optimal hygiene conditions before feeding the wide bellies of the pot-stills* in November and throughout the winter.

Vintages

In cognac country, the spirit's year of production does not usually appear on the label.

A modern horizontal press.

Coming out of the barrel, the cognac has taken on its beautiful amber color.

A cognac's color is one of the signs of its quality.

In general, you will only find partial information, which may appear more or less esoteric. Acronyms and terms that are used include V.O. (very old), V.S.O.P. (very superior old pale) and Vieille Réserve (old reserve), which generally indicate that the final product contains brandies no younger than *compte* 4, which means they are more than four years old. Extra, Napoleon, and X.O. (extra old) contain brandies with at least *compte* 6. At this point, we should also mention some of the other denominations used by the profession*, all of which have a note of fantasy to them: Rare & Delicate, Cordon Bleu, Très Belle (Very Beautiful), Vénérable, Séléction des Anges (Angels' Selection), Réserve, Ancestrale, Antique, Triomphe, and Family Reserve. These names have been dreamt up by firms as marketing terms in order to distinguish their different products.

Note also that the official designations (V.S.O.P., X.O., etc.) constitute only a guarantee of the minimum time the cognac has spent in a cask, and for some brands it will actually have been in the cask for much longer periods. Otard's Napoleon, for example, is fifteen years old; X.O. thirty-five years old; and Extra is fifty to sixty years old. To indicate a vintage year would be to deprive the producer of a whole range of blending*

JAS HENNESSY & Co
Cognac France
Hennessy
COGNAC
FINE
de
COGNAC
QUALITE RARE
JAS HENNESSY & Co
Cognac France
40%vol
e70cl

possibilities, notably in the large houses, which can have a vast array of brandies in reserve. Unless there is an indication of the bottling date (recommended by the profession), a vintage date is more or less a contested piece of information, since a thirty-year-old bottle* could very well contain a cognac that only spent five years in cask and was "stopped" in its evolution when bottled.

Since 1998, when authorization was given allowing the separate aging* of batches* of raw brandy, subject to strict controls and precise dating, small owner-grower-distillers, who market their product under their own brand names, have begun to market vintage cognacs. They affirm their desire to shake up consumers and to distinguish themselves from the major traditional firms, some of which might be resting a bit on the laurels of their long-standing reputations. Not having the same diversity of products, these producers favor a "hand-produced" approach to the quality, aging, and storing of their products. They claim, perhaps rather boldly, that they have an originality capable of at least stimulating the market, if not exactly overturning the established hierarchy.

Water

To speak about water in the country of cognac could appear paradoxical, or even provocative. Let's not forget, however, that the first goal of cognac production was to concentrate wine, reducing it to alcohol by distillation*, so that shippers could use water to reconstitute it in another place. The objective was, on one hand, to allow it to travel without deteriorating and, on the other, to lower the cost of transport by reducing the volume of the alcohol. We should note that today many of the major firms focus their publicity on serving their product with water, as was once the case when *fine* à l'eau* was still fashionable. To combat the effects of a worrying overproduction, some have even produced special cognacs for this purpose. "Cognac with water is back" could almost be a slogan for the profession*.

The word cognac inevitably brings to mind the River Charente*; this waterway was for many years indispensable to the transportation of the spirit. With the nearby ocean bringing all the rain needed for its vines, the region's rainfall is well able to feed this scale of river—it is not the Amazon!—regularly.

Facing in a westerly direction, the coast always offered seafarers the shelter of its islands and the haven of its ports. So it is hardly surprising that bold navigators arrived from afar—Vikings from the North, Arabs from the south, and merchants from England and the New World.

At first, many came in search of salt, which was produced by the evaporation of seawater. It was not long before these visitors were taking an interest in the wine and, as it did not travel well, they imagined reducing it to produce a stronger alcohol. Cognac, also known as *eau-de-vie* or "water of life" certainly merits the term, as it continues to be the mainstay of 55 percent of the region's active rural population, some 22,000 Charentais.

A hauling path is a reminder of former times, when men and animals dragged barges up the River Charente.

ADDRESSES

BUREAU NATIONAL INTERPROFESSIONNEL DU COGNAC (BNIC)
23, allées du Champ de Mars
16100 Cognac
Tel.: +33 (0)5 45 35 60 00
Fax: +33 (0)5 45 82 86 54
www.bnic.fr

CHARENTE DEPARTMENT TOURISM COMMITTEE
Place de la Gare
16000 Angoulême
Tel.: +33 (0)5 45 92 27 57
www.lacharente.com

CHARENTE-MARITIME DEPARTMENT TOURISM COMMITTEE
11bis, rue des Augustins
17000 La Rochelle
Tel.: +33 (0)5 46 41 43 33
www.charente-maritime.org

COGNAC MUSEUM
46, boulevard Denfert-Rochereau
16100 Cognac
Tel.: +33 (0)5 45 32 07 27

COGNAC TOURISM OFFICE
14, rue du 14 juillet
16100 Cognac
Tel.: +33 (0)5 45 82 10 71
www.tourism-cognac.com

COMITÉ NATIONAL DU PINEAU DES CHARENTES
112, avenue Victor Hugo
16100 Cognac
Tel: +33 (0)5 45 32 09 27
Fax: +33 (0)5 45 35 42 25
www.pineau.fr

POITOU-CHARENTES REGIONAL TOURISM COMMITTEE
2, rue Sainte-Opportune
86002 Poitiers
Tel.: +33 (0)5 49 88 38 94
www.poitou-charentes-vacances.com

QUAIS HENNESSY
1, rue de la Richonne
(Wilmotte building)
16101 Cognac Cedex
Tel.: +33 (0)5 45 35 72 72

UNIVERSITÉ INTERNATIONALE DES EAUX-DE-VIE ET BOISSONS SPIRITEUSES (TRAINING ORGANIZATION)
Centre universitaire
de la Charente – Segonzac Site
37, rue Gaston Briand
16130 Segonzac
Tel.: +33 (0)5 45 83 35 35
Fax: +33 (0)5 45 83 31 72

COGNAC APPELLATION D'ORIGINE CONTRÔLÉE TERMINOLOGY

Cognac
Fine Cognac
Eau-de-vie de Cognac
Eau-de-vie des Charantes
Grande Champagne or Grande Fine Champagne: 100% Grande Champagne brandy
Petite Champagne or Petite Fine Champagne: 100% Petite Champagne brandy
Fine Champagne: blend of Grande and Petite Champagne brandies with a minimum of 50% Grande Champagne
Borderies or Fines Borderies: 100% Borderies brandy
Fins Bois or Fine Fins Bois: 100% Fins Bois brandy
Bons Bois or Fine Bons Bois: 100% Bons Bois brandy

COGNAC HARVESTS

Total harvest of white cognac wines (2000): 215,237,862 gallons (8,147,641 hl)

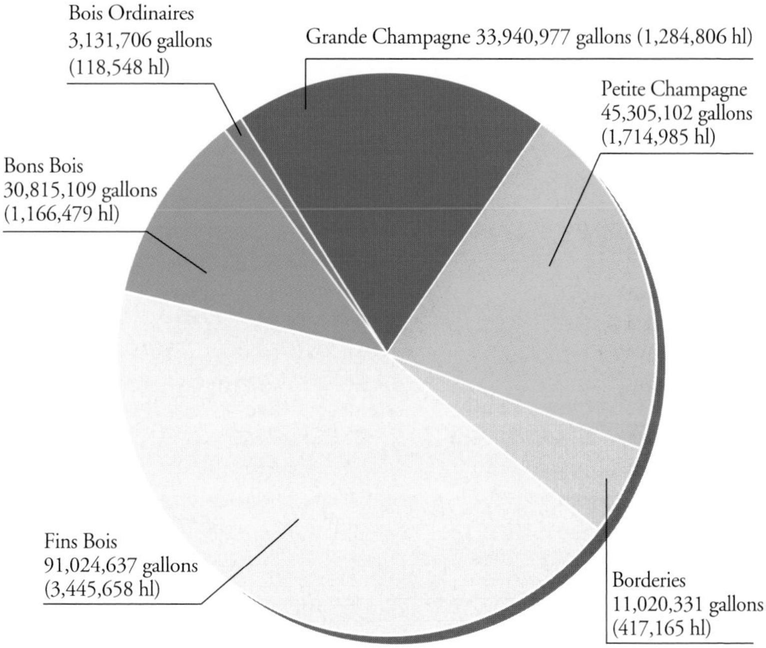

Bois Ordinaires
3,131,706 gallons
(118,548 hl)
Grande Champagne 33,940,977 gallons (1,284,806 hl)
Petite Champagne
45,305,102 gallons
(1,714,985 hl)
Bons Bois
30,815,109 gallons
(1,166,479 hl)
Fins Bois
91,024,637 gallons
(3,445,658 hl)
Borderies
11,020,331 gallons
(417,165 hl)

COGNAC DISTILLATION: SOME FIGURES

Production in thousands of hectolitres* of pure alcohol
800
600
400
200
380 049 hl
82
84
86
88
90
92
94
96
98
00/01

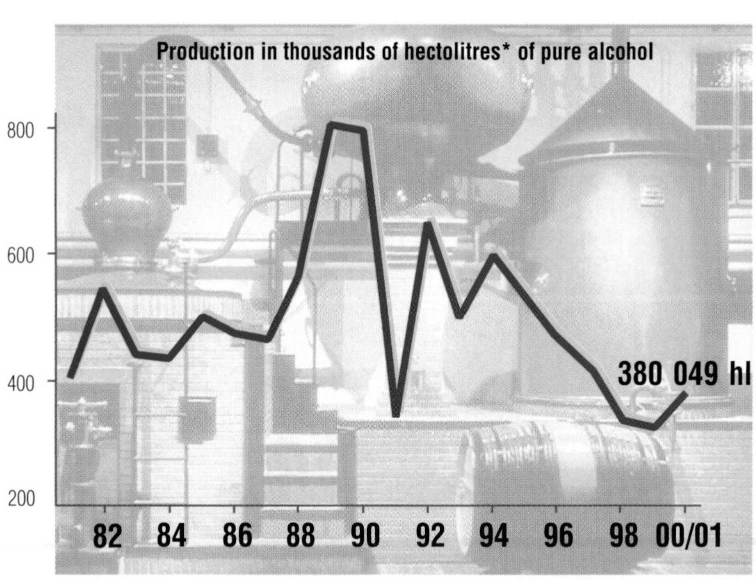

SELECTED COGNAC BRANDS AND PRODUCERS

NAMES	PRODUCTS
l'Abbaye, Les raisins de 17, chemin de l'Abbaye 17400 Asnières-la-Giraud	V.S., V.S.O.P., Vieille Réserve
Philippe et Claude-Marie Arrivé L'Augerie 17240 Champagnolles	Cognac cru Bons Bois, Three-star, Galon Bleu, Troisième Millénaire
Jean-Yves Audebert-Valtaud Le Bois de Vaux 16170 Vaux-Rouillac	Three-star, V.S.O.P., Vieille Réserve, X.O.
Augier Robin Briand & Co. 36, rue Gabriel Jaulin 16102 Cognac Cedex	Classique, V.S.O.P. Champagne
Jean Balluet 1, rue des Ardillères 17490 Neuvicq-le-Château	Fine cognac, Très vieille réserve
Banchereau Puits Mesnard 16120 Éraville	Napoléon, X.O. Extra Old
Barbeau et Fils Les Vignes 17160 Sonnac	Fine cognac Three-star, Vieille Réserve, Très vieux cognac
Veuve Baron et Fils Logis de Brissac 16370 Cherves-Richemont	V.S.O.P., Napoléon, Hors d'Âge
Paul Beau 18, rue Millardet 16130 Segonzac	Grande Champagne V.S.O.P., Hors d'Âge, Extra Vieille
Bisquit (Renault-Bisquit) Domaine des Lignières 16170 Cognac Cedex	Classique, V.S.O.P. Fine Champagne, Napoléon Fine Champagne
Domaine de Beaulieu 16300 Lamérac	V.S.O.P., X.O., Old Vintage Magnum X.O.
Yves Beaumont Chai Marronnier 17130 Rouffignac	Bons Bois
Bernard Bégaud La Métairie de la Barre 17770 Villars-les-Bois	Spécial Tonic, Sélection, Mes 20 ans, Prince Noir, Grand-Père Gabriel

SELECTED COGNAC BRANDS AND PRODUCERS

Bel Ange 2, rue du Foyer Meussac 17800 Échebrune	V.S., X.O., Extra
Raymond Bellebeau 2, rue de l'ouche gué Les Brousses 17490 Neuvicq-le-Château	Fine cognac three-star, V.S.O.P., Vieille Réserve
Alain Blanchard Lasdoux 16120 Angeac-Charente	Long Drink, Petite Champagne : V.S.O.P., X.O.
Claude Boisselet 17260 Givrezac	V.S.O.P., X.O., Eden, Millénium
Boule et Fils La Verrerie 17150 Boisredon	Cordifolin, Three-star, V.S.O.P., Napoléon, X.O.
Daniel Bouffard Chez Bouchet 17520 Sainte-Lheurine	Cognac as an apéritif Cognac for Charentais coffee
Bouju (Daniel Bouju) Saint-Preuil 16130 Segonzac	Grande Champagne Empereur, Extra, Très vieux brut de fût, Cuisine
Pierre Boullmer 19, rue du Palais 16100 Cognac	V.S., V.S.O.P., X.O., Grande Champagne 1er grand cru
Louis Bouron (Château de la Grange) 189, avenue de Jarnac 17416 Saint-Jean-d'Angély	Three-star, Prestige, Blason d'Or, X.O., Très Vieille Réserve
Branchaud La Gasconnière 17500 Ozillac	V.S., V.S.O.P., X.O.
Brillet (Jean-Louis Brillet) Les Aireaux 16120 Graves	Réserve, Très vieille réserve, Grande et Petite Champagne
Joan Brisson 7, rue de Saint-Hérie 17160 Matha	Long Drink, Three-star

SELECTED COGNAC BRANDS AND PRODUCERS

Producer	Cognacs
Freddy Brun Chez Babœuf 16300 Barret	Petite Champagne : V.S.O.P., X.O.
Guy Brunetaux Chez Filhon 16300 Montchaude	Fine Petite Champagne (61°)
Camus 29, rue Marguerite de Navarre BP 19 16100 Cognac	Grand V.S.O.P., Napoléon Vieille Réserve, X.O., Extra, Borderies X.O.
Chabanneau (C.G.E.V.F.) 29, rue Marguerite de Navarre 16100 Cognac	V.S., V.S.O.P., Napoléon, X.O.
Chabasse 47, rue Élysée Loustalot 17412 Saint-Jean	V.S.O.P. Napoléon, X.O., X.O. Impérial, Baccarat
Alain Chadutaud Bourras 16200 Mérignac	Cognac for cooking and flambéing
Bertrand Chadutaud Route de Fleurac 16200 Mérignac	Three-star, V.S.O.P., X.O.
Chainier Dominique et Fils La Barde Fagnouse 17520 Arthenac	Petite Champagne Fine Champagne, X.O., Grande Champagne
Chapelle Sonneville Chantecaille 16130 Lignières-Sonneville	V.S., V.S.O.P., Napoléon, X.O.
Château de Beaulon 25, rue Saint-Vincent 17240 Saint-Dizant-du-Gua	Cognac Rare sélections 1904, 1907, 1914
Couillaud (EARL Les Côteaux de Montignac) 3, route de Fontgrand 17800 Bougneau	Le Brûlot Charentais (60°) Long Drink, Three-star, X.O., Réserve
Rémy Couillebaud G.A.E.C. du Maine Ormeau–Le Cluzeau 16290 Moulidars	Three-star, V.S.O.P., Napoléon, Vieille réserve

SELECTED COGNAC BRANDS AND PRODUCERS

Couprie S.A.R.L.
La Roumade
16300 Ambleville

Séléction du Domaine, V.S.O.P., Napoléon, X.O., Hors d'Âge

Courvoisier S.A.
2, place du Château
16200 Jarnac

V.S., V.S.O.P. Fine Champagne, Napoléon, X.O. Impérial, Initiale Extra, Erté n° 7

Croizet (Cognac Pierre Croizet)
Lantin
16200 Triac-Lautrait

V.S.O.P., X.O., Napoléon, Carafe, Cristal, Vintage cognacs

Jean Claude Danjou
Allée des Vieux Peupliers–Goux
17800 Pérignac

Non-denatured cognacs for culinary use

Delamain
7, rue J. & R. Delamain
16200 Jarnac

Pale & Dry, Vesper, Très Vénérable, Réserve de la Famille, Vintage cognacs

Jacques Denis
Les Pouges
16130 Saint-Preuil

V.S.O.P. Premier cru X.O., Extra Grande Champagne, Tonic Saveur

Jean Claude Dhiersat
Le Breuil
16170 Rouillac

Three-star, V.S.O.P., Napoléon, Très Vieille Réserve

Maison A.E. Dor
4, bis rue Jacques Moreau
16200 Jarnac

Sélection, V.S.O.P., Napoléon, Vieille Fine Champagne, X.O.

Dupuy Bache Gabrielsen
32, rue de Boston
16100 Cognac

Three-star, X.O., Fine Champagne, Hors d'Âge

Fillioux Fils
La Pouyade
16130 Juillac-le-Coq

La Pouyade, Cep d'Or and Golf X.O. Impérial, Cigare Club, Family reserve

La Fine Goule
Pimbert
17520 Arthenac

V.S.O.P., Napoléon, Réserve, Hors d'Âge, Très Vieux

Forgeron Michel
Chez Richon
16130 Segonzac

Three-star, V.S.O.P., Vieille Réserve, Hors d'Âge, Cognac for flambéing

P. Frapin & Co.
Rue Pierre Frapin
16130 Segonzac

V.S. Luxe, V.S.O.P., VIP X.O., Château Fontpinot, Extra, Vintage 1983, Rabelais

SELECTED COGNAC BRANDS AND PRODUCERS

A. de Fusigny 232, place Jean Monnet 16200 Jarnac	Sélection, V.S.O.P., X.O., Ebony, Cigare Blend, Fine Champagne, Très Vieille Grande Champagne
F. Gacon 17160 Les Touches-de-Périgny	V.S., Three-star, V.S.O.P., Napoléon, X.O.
Jules Gaufret (Unicognac) Route de Cognac 17500 Jonzac	Three-star, V.S.O.P., 10 years, X.O., 2000, Ona, Gastronomie
Henri Geffard La Chambre 16130 Verrières	Three-star, V.S.O.P., Vieille Réserve, Très Vieux
François Giboin L'Hermitage 16370 Cherves-Richemont	Sélection V.S., V.S.O.P., Réserve de l'Hermitage, Napoléon, X.O. Royal
Paul Giraud et Fils Le Bourg 16120 Bouteville	V.S.O.P. Premier cru cognac Napoléon Grande Champagne, Vieille Réserve X.O., Très Rare
Godet Frères 1, rue du Duc 17000 La Rochelle	Three-star or V.S., V.S.O.P., Napoléon, X.O.
Gourry de Chadeville 16130 Segonzac	Grande Fine Champage, X.O., Très Vieux
Grégor 47, rue Aliénor d'Aquitaine 17610 Chaniers	Vieille Réserve, X.O., Hors d'Âge
L. & M. Grimaud 4, rue de Port Boutiers 16100 Boutiers-Saint-Trojan	Gold Sensation, V.S. Élégance, V.S.O.P. Qualité Rare, X.O., Créature and Très Vieille Réserve
Guerbé & Co. Hameau de l'Échalotte 16130 Juillac-le-Coq	Pub Blend, V.S. Grande Champagne, Napoléon, Grande Champagne, Rare Réserve, X.O.
Hennessy 1, rue de la Richonne 16100 Cognac	V.S, Hennessy Pure White, Hennessy Fine de Cognac, X.O, Private Reserve, Paradis Extra, Richard Hennessy, Timeless

SELECTED COGNAC BRANDS AND PRODUCERS

Producer	Brands
Thomas Hine & Co. 16, quai de l'Orangerie 16200 Jarnac	Rare & Delicate, Antique Triomphe, Family Reserve, Vintage cognacs
JLF (EARL du Chail) Chez Dexmier 16130 Ars	Drinker (for long drink), V.S. Séduction, V.S.O.P.
Philippe Laclie 3, chemin des Noyers 17770 Bercloux	V.S., V.S.O.P., Vieille Réserve, X.O. Laclie
Alain Ladrat Malbrac 16200 Jarnac	Réserve, Napoléon X.O.
Jean-Pierre Lambert Place du Champ de Foire 16370 Cherves-Richemont	Cognac des Borderies Three-star et V.S.O.P., Réserve, Vieille Réserve
Rémi Landier Cors 16200 Foussignac	V.S. Three-star, Sélection, V.S.O.P., Napoléon, X.O., Vieille Réserve, Extra
Henri de Lotherie Beauregard 16130 Juillac-le-Coq	Grande Champagne : Cognac « O » Long Drink, Vieille Réserve, X.O.
Maine-Giraud 16250 Champagne-Vigny	Three-star, V.S.O.P., Vieille Réserve
Simone Marcadier Le Pible 16130 Segonzac	V.S. Spécial Long Drink V.S.O.P., Napoléon, X.O., Vieille Réserve
Patrice Marchand Les Moulineaux 17150 St-Bonnet-sur-Gironde	Three-star V.S.O.P., X.O., Napoléon
Marnier, Lapostolle 16200 Bourg-Charente	V.S., V.S.O.P., X.O.
Maison Martell & Co. 7, place Édouard Martell 16100 Cognac	V.S., V.S.O.P., Noblige, Napoléon Special Reserve, Cordon Bleu, X.O. Suprème
J.P. Menard et Fils 2, rue de la Cure 16720 St-Même-les-Carrières	Sélection des Domaines, V.S.O.P., Napoléon, Réserve X.O., Ancestrale

SELECTED COGNAC BRANDS AND PRODUCERS

Producer	Brands
Menuet (Eurocognac) La Tonnelle 16720 St-Même-les-Carrières	V.S.O.P., 10 year-old, X.O., Extra
Laurent Merlin Chez Pineau 17520 Arthenac	Fine Petite Champagne
Claude and Jeanine Moulin 6, rue des Vallées 17490 Macqueville	Sélection, V.S.O.P., Napoléon, Vieille Réserve, X.O.
Jacques Ordonneau Domaine de la Grolette 16370 Cherves-Richemont	V.S. des Borderies, V.S.O.P. des Borderies Très Vieille Réserve
Otard Château de Cognac 127, boulevard Denfert-Rochereau 16100 Cognac	V.S., V.S.O.P., Napoléon, X.O. Gold, Otard 55, Otard 1795
Jean Paynaud (SARL Du Peux) Les Gauthiers 16120 Bouteville	Premier cru cognac : Sélection, Napoléon, Vieille Réserve
Dominique Perraud Chez Barrand 17500 Champagnac	Cognac Long Drink
André Petit et Fils Le Bourg 16480 Berneuil	Three-star, V.S.O.P., Vieille Réserve Napoléon, Very rare X.O., Hors d'Âge
François Peyrot Marancheville 16200 Gondeville	Three-star, Napoléon, X.O., Héritage
Frédéric Pierre Les Grands Champs 16130 Segonzac	V.S., V.S.O.P., Extra, Vieille Réserve, X.O.
Distillerie du Peyrat 4, impasse des Alambics Le Peyrat 16200 Houlette	V.S. (tonic), V.S.O.P., EXTRA
François Peyrot Marancheville 16200 Gondeville	Three-star, Napoléon, X.O., Héritage

SELECTED COGNAC BRANDS AND PRODUCERS

Producer	Brands
Planat (C.G.E.V.F.) 29, rue Marguerite de Navarre 16100 Cognac	V.S., V.S.O.P., Napoléon, X.O.
Domaine du Plantis 36, rue du Plantis 17160 Courcerac	Long Drink, V.S.O.P., Napoléon, X.O.
Félix Poussard Le Petit Essart 16100 Javrezac	Sélection Three-star, V.S.O.P. Borderies, Fine Napoléon
Prince de Didonne Vignerons Côtes de Saintonge Château de Didonne 17120 Semussac	Three-star, V.S.O.P., Napoléon, X.O.
Prince Hubert de Polignac Henri Mounier 49, rue Lohmeyer 16100 Cognac	Three-star, V.S.O.P.
Prunier Henri Mounier 49, rue Lohmeyer 16102 Cognac Cedex	V.S., V.S.O.P., Family Reserve 20 Years Old X.O. Très Vieille Grande Champagne
Raymond Ragnaud Le Château 16300 Ambleville	Réserve Grande Champagne, Sélection, Héritage, Très Vieille Grande Champagne, Hors d'Âge, Extra Vieux (X.O.)
Ragnaud - Sabourin La Voûte 16300 Ambleville	Alliance Grande Champagne no. 4 GC, no. 10 V.S.O.P., no. 20 Réserve Spéciale, X.O.
Rémy Martin & Co. 20, rue de la Société Vinicole 16100 Cognac	V.S.O.P., X.O., Extra, Louis XIII
Rénier (Cognac Charpentron) Le Clos de Mérienne 16700 Gondeville	V.S.O.P., Napoléon, X.O., Hors d'Âge
Gyl Richard 5, rue de la Rente–Figers 17800 Échebrune	V.S., V.S.O.P., X.O., Extra
Roullet & Fils Le Goulet 16200 Foussignac	V.S., V.S.O.P. Réserve, Vieille Réserve Napoléon, Extra Grande Champagne

SELECTED COGNAC BRANDS AND PRODUCERS

Producer	Brands
Rumeau et Fils Domaine Les "Quillets" 16250 Champagne-Vigny	Three-star, V.S.O.P., Napoléon, X.O.
Seguinot & Co. La Nérolle 16130 Segonzac	V.S.O.P., X.O., Âge Inconnu Héritage
Guy Testaud 16300 Lamérac	V.S.O.P., Napoléon, X.O., Héritage, Excellence, 1973
Henriette Thomas Rue Maurice Sellal 16100 St-Laurent-de-Cognac	Cognac as an apéritif, V.S.O.P.
Claude Thorin Chez Boujut 16200 Mainxe	Séduction, V.S.O.P., Napoléon, X.O., Héritage, Princeps, X.O. Royal
Château de la Tillade 17260 St-Simon-de-Pellouaille	V.S., V.S.O.P., X.O.
Jean Vallade 37, route des Charmilles 17520 Brie-sous-Archiac	V.S. Sélection, V.S.O.P., Napoléon
Jean-Marie Vallaeys Rippe 17270 Montguyon	Three-star « Apéro » Three-star, V.S.O.P., Extra Vieux
Vallein Tercinier Domaine des Forges 17460 Chermignac	Sélection, V.S.O.P., Napoléon, Grande Champagne, Petite Champagne, Fins Bois, Bons Bois, Hors d'Âge, Millénaire
Bernard Vaudon Villars-Marange 16200 Jarnac	V.S., V.S.O.P., Napoléon
du Véron Place de l'Eglise 16370 Mesnac	V.S., X.O. Perle d'Or, X.O. Collection Privilège, X.O. Vieille Réserve
François Voyer Le Maine-Verret 16130 Verrières	V.S.O.P., Napoléon, X.O., Extra

The addresses found on this non-exhaustive list come from the Bureau National Interprofessionnel du Cognac's web site—www.bnic.fr. The selection of firms was made based on the diversity and originality of their products and the amount of information provided by the site. Despite the care taken in compiling this list, neither the author nor the publisher can be held responsible for possible omissions or errors.

SELECTED BIBLIOGRAPHY

Behrendt, Axel and Bibiana. *Cognac.* New York: Abbeville Press, 1997. Translated from German by Russel Stockman.

Brown, Gordon. *Handbook of Fine Brandies.* Garamond Publishers, 1990.

Calabrese, Salvatore. *Cognac.* Sterling Publications, 2002.

Cullen, Louis. Brandy T*rade under the Ancien Regime: Regional Specialization in the Charente.* Cambridge University Press, 2002.

Delos, Gilbert. T*he World of Cognac.* Book Sales, 1999.

Faith, Nicolas. Classic Brandy. London: Trafalgar Square, 2000.

Gregory, Conal R. The Cognac Companion: A Connoisseurs Guide. Philadelphia: Running Press, 1999.

MacAndrew, A. Cognac, *An Independent Guide to the People, the Product and the Region.* Lusina Publishing, 1999.

McNulty, Henry. *The Vogue Cocktail Book.* New York: Crown Publishing, 1984.

Pacault, F. Paul. *Kindred Spirits.* Hyperion, 1997.

Ray, Cyril. *Cognac.* London: Peter Davies, 1973.

Spencer, Herbert. *Cognac Country.* London: Quiller Press, 1983.

Photographic credits: BNIC 36 bottom, 38, 42 top, 42-43 bottom, 43 top, 45 top, 46, 47, 63 top, 64-65 bottom, 68, 70, 80 bottom, 83 bottom, 100, 102-103 bottom, 108; BNIC/Thierry Blay 55; BNIC/Jean-Yves Boyer 27, 39, 41 top, 49 bottom, 51 bottom left, 73 bottom; BNIC/Burdin 48 bottom, 48-49 top, 98; BNIC/J. Clavel 71; BNIC/Alain Danvers 22 top, 60-61, 72 bottom, 104; BNIC/Stéphane Graciès 89; BNIC/Paul Heidelberg 66; BNIC/Jean-François Poussard 1, 28 top, 51 bottom right, 84 bottom, 86; BNIC/Livio Senigaliesi 50; BNIC/Jean Daniel Sudres 4–5; BNIC/Bernard Verrax 10, 13 top, 16 top, 20-21, 22 bottom, 25, 26 top, 26 bottom, 40-41, 58 top, 59 top, 63 bottom, 64-65 top, 65 bottom, 78 bottom, 78-79, 84 top, 87, 90, 96-97; Comité National du Pineau des Charantes 81; Burdin/CNPC 2 bottom, 82 top, back cover bottom; Document Les Cours 75 top, 93, 94; Jas Hennessy & Co. collection/historical collection 12, 14, 15 top, 17 top, 23, 24, 44–45 bottom, 56, 69 top, 91, 92; Hennessy & Co./Mirco Braccini 2 top, 2 middle, 18, 30, 31, 34 bottom, 35, 36-37 top, 51 top, 52, 53, 62, 67, 83 top; Hennessy & Co./Peter Knaup 105; Hennessy & Co./Guy Knowell 11; Hennessy & Co./Les Ateliers Martron 19, 21 top, 34 top, 37 bottom, 69 bottom, 77 bottom, 94-95 bottom, 95 top, 99 bottom, 99 top, 110 bottom (photo), front cover; Hennessy & Co./Dominique Ravelo 6, 7 top, 7 bottom, 8 top, 8 bottom, 9 top, 9 bottom, 13 bottom, 15 bottom, 16 middle, 33, 58, 59 bottom, 73 top, 74, 75 bottom, 76 bottom, 76-77 top, 80 top, 88, 97 top, 101, 102, 106-107, back cover top and middle; Nicolas 32, 79 bottom. Tables and maps: BNIC 20 top, 54, 85 top, 85 bottom, 97 bottom, 110 bottom (graph), 110 top, inside front cover; Editions Larmat 28 bottom, 29.

The author and the publisher would like to thank Hennessy for providing information and access to documents, as well as the Bureau Interprofessionnel du Cognac (BNIC), the Comité National du Pineau des Charentes, and the company Nicolas for their kind participation.

Translated and adapted from the French by Anne Trager
Copy-editing: Kate van den Boogert
Typesetting: Claude Olivier-Four
Color separation: Les Cours–Caen

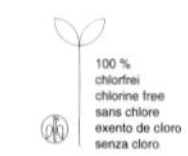

Originally published as *L'ABCdaire du Cognac*

ISBN: 2-0801-1075-6
FA1075-02-IX
Dépot legal: 9/2002
Printed and bound by Pollina S.A., France n° L87963